S0-BQT-069

BS
1450
20th
.R6513
1991

THE *TRACTATUS SUPER PSALMUM VICESIMUM* OF RICHARD ROLLE OF HAMPOLE

James C. Dolan

Texts and Studies in Religion
Volume 57

The Edwin Mellen Press
Lewiston/Queenston/Lampeter

HIEBERT LIBRARY   35/24
Fresno Pacific College - M. B. Seminary
Fresno, Calif 93702

Library of Congress Cataloging-in-Publication Data

This work has been registered with the Library of Congress

This is volume 57 in the continuing series
Texts and Studies in Religion
Volume 57 ISBN 0-7734-9666-1
TSR Series ISBN 0-88946-976-8

A CIP catalog record for this book
is available from the British Library.

Copyright ©1991 James C. Dolan

All rights reserved. For information contact

The Edwin Mellen Press   The Edwin Mellen Press
Box 450   Box 67
Lewiston, New York   Queenston, Ontario
USA 14092   CANADA L0S 1L0

The Edwin Mellen Press, Ltd.
Lampeter, Dyfed, Wales
UNITED KINGDOM SA48 7DY

Printed in the United States of America

For my mother
and
in memory of my father

TABLE OF CONTENTS

ACKNOWLEDGEMENTS

My work on this text goes back a number of years, and I remember with great affection those men whose character and example as teachers and scholars drew me to the study of the medieval mystics and the delightful labor of text editing--and kept me going despite the many slings and arrows. First among them is Gilbert G. Wright, my mentor at the University of Illinois, whose generosity and steady support has never flagged--even when it probably should have. Richard Hamilton Greene, regretfully, did not live to see this volume, but memories of his quiet wisdom and grace under pressure will long outlast it.

More recently, Nicholas J. Watson of the University of Western Ontario, my friend and colleague in the study of Rolle, deserves special thanks: his spirit not only gave me the energy to finish the work, but it keeps fresh in my mind the ideals that once brought me to the profession of letters.

I also wish to thank the American Philosophical Society, the American Council of Learned Societies, and the University of Illinois Graduate Research Fund for their financial support for my initial research; and the Bodleian Library, Corpus Christi College Library, Oxford; Corpus Christi College Library, Cambridge; the library of Lincoln Cathedral; and University Library of Uppsala for microfilms of their manuscripts. I must recognize the warmth, consideration, and professional expertise of Alice Rivers and Douglas Flaming of the Edwin Mellen Press. And finally, to my wife Diane, who sometimes lost sight of me during the stretch run, *aere perennius* my love and thanks for always being there.

J.C.D.

INTRODUCTION

I

The Tradition

The text of the *Tractatus super Psalmum Vicesimum*, which is extant in six manuscripts and one edition printed from a manuscript still unidentified, is here presented in its first modern edition.

The *Tractatus super Psalmum Vicesimum* of Richard Rolle of Hampole is an example of English biblical commentary written during the first half of the Fourteenth Century. But far from being just another example of tropological exegesis, this short piece is especially interesting for the insight it provides into the uses, other than the simple explanation of a text, to which the commentary form can be adapted; it does explain a text, and very lucidly, but it also embodies the spiritual advice and exhortation of a master to his disciples, above all reflecting the point of view and personal experience of its author in a style that is both forceful and controlled. If the *Tractatus* is not therefore a literary work, it comes very close to being so.

The Biography

Richard Rolle, although well known as a spiritual writer and mystic for well over a century after his death--over four hundred manuscripts remain in libraries throughout England and the Continent and editions of his works were being printed up to 1677--did not leave us much reliable information about his life. The currently accepted biography of Rolle is highly tentative because it rests on unreliable sources and on autobiographical hints gleaned from his works, most of which have not yet been critically edited or chronologically ordered.

The main source of biographical information is the *Officium* and *Miracula* prepared for the Cistercian nuns of Hampole Priory in anticipation of Rolle's canonization, an event which did not materialize.[1] If we balance the *Officium* against what local records tell us of Yorkshire history and Rolle's contemporaries, we are able to construct a pattern of life that appears realistic and commensurate with the most trustworthy facts. To be specific, we know on the testimony of too many manuscripts to question its validity that Rolle died in 1349. The facts surrounding his birth are confused by the difficulty of identifying the "William Rolle" mentioned in the *Officium* as his father with any of the Rolles in the Yorkshire records and by the equally frustrating fact that there are many candidates for the place of his birth, a certain "*villa de Thornton Eboracensis diocesis.*"[2]

Judging from what little we know of the lives of those most intimately associated with Rolle, his patrons Thomas de Neville and John de Dalton, he

---

[1] The *Officium de Sancto Ricardo de Hampole* was edited by G. G. Perry as EETS (Original Series No. 20), 1867 and later in the *York Breviary*, Surtees Society 75, ii. App. V., 1882. This version was reprinted by Canon R. M. Wooley as *The Officium and Miracula of Richard Rolle of Hampole* (London: Society for Promoting Christian Knowledge, 1919). An abridged copy of the work was printed by Harold Lindkvist, *Skrifter utgifna af K. Humanistiska Vetenskaps*, xix. 3, Upsala, 1917.

[2] There is still much confusion about which Yorkshire village is meant. Bodley MS. e Musaeo 193 (Sum. Cat. No. 3610), ff. 3^v–34 contains the addition "*iuxta Pickering*" in a hand described as c. 1450–75. This could be Thornton Dale, but the lack of further manuscript support and the fact that there are several Thorntons near Pickering make its validity uncertain. Still, C. Horstman in *Yorkshire Writers: Richard Rolle of Hampole and His Followers*, 2 vols. (London, 1896), II, v–vi accepts it although he also accepts the suggestion of H. R. Bramley, *The Psalter or Psalms of David and Certain Canticles with a Translation and Exposition in English by Richard Rolle of Hampole* (Oxford, 1884), p. vi, n. that Thornton was "possibly at Topcliffe near Thirsk." For the best discussion of the question, see Hope Emily Allen, *Writings Ascribed to Richard Rolle Hermit of Hampole and Materials for His Biography* (New York, 1927), 430–444.

must have been born at, or shortly after[3], the turn of the century. At a suitable age (*"opportuno tempore"*), probably about thirteen,[4] he went up to Oxford with the patronage of Thomas de Neville, later archdeacon of Durham (1334), with the desire to be instructed rather in *"theologicis sacra scripture quam phisicis aut secularis scientie disciplinis."*[5] Though he did not stay for the degree, his works show that he had learned enough theology to handle some of the complex questions of the day.[6] At some point before the degree, according to the *Officium* *"decimo nono vite sue anno considerans tempus vite mortalis incertum et terminum tremebundum,"* Rolle returned home determined to lead the holy life of a hermit.

As the often-quoted story has it, he borrowed from his sister two tunics, one gray, one white, and took his father's rain hood from which he

---

[3] For the most recent argument on Rolle's date of birth, see the book on Rolle by Professor Nicholas J. Watson, forthcoming in late 1991, the manuscript of which he has been kind enough to share with me.

[4] Allen (444-5) quotes H. Rashdall, *Universities of Europe in the Middle Ages* (Oxford, 1895), I, 461 to the effect that "twenty was recorded as the minimum age for mastership, and the full course in the Arts was seven years. Thirteen was therefore the normal age for admission. . . . We are told that the system of teaching was exactly the same in Oxford as in Paris (II, 460), and therefore Neville may have been a master by twenty, and able to give effectual support to a boy of thirteen just coming up."

[5] Oxford was in its heyday of scholasticism at this time; Duns Scotus had been lecturing there from 1297-1301. Cf. "Duns Scotus," *New Catholic Encyclopedia*, 1967, IV, 1102 seq.

[6] Several of Rolle's works show a detailed knowledge of theological subjects; the *Latin Psalter, Super Orationem Dominicam*, and *Super Symbolum Apostolorum* contain "occasional careful reasoning on theological subjects" (*Allen* 448). Dom Noetinger in an article entitled "The Biography of Richard Rolle," *The Month* (January, 1926) expresses his conviction that Rolle was a skilled theologian. Be that as it may, in the *Job* Rolle argues many points with great care and thoroughness and gives a wider theological treatment than in any other Scripture-based work.

made a garment resembling the traditional hermit's garb.[7] When his sister
saw what he was doing, she thought he had gone mad so he was forced to flee
to the woods (*"nemus vicinum"*) for the solitude he desired. On the vigil of
the Assumption (August 15th) the sons of the Dalton family discovered him
praying in the family's chapel. The next morning, having obtained the
priest's permission, Rolle preached such an eloquent sermon from the pulpit
that John de Dalton invited him to dinner at which he honored Rolle with a
place at table above his own sons. At first disturbed by Rolle's retirement
from the world without parental permission but finally convinced of the
holiness of his intentions, Dalton offered to become Rolle's patron. Rolle
accepted and for some time received from Dalton the necessities of life and a
"locum mansionis solitarie" in or near the Dalton house.

From this point in the biography the *Officium* is colored by its purpose
of furthering Rolle's canonization. The lectiones describe events of a
miraculous character: the *"domina domus,"* presumably Lady Dalton, and
several of her friends paid Rolle a visit while he was writing; he spoke to
them on spiritual topics for two hours without laying down his pen or
dropping a word. During his early period of mystical experience he was
tempted by the apparition of a beautiful young woman whom he had known
"in good love."[8] He cured a "certain woman" near whose home he had his

----

[7] The *Officium* (Wooley 23) records that Rolle *"ea accepisset illico manicas grisee
tunice detruncavit et albe tunice botones abscidit. et modo quo poterat albe tunice manicas
consuit."* In the *Miracula* (84), leccio v tells us that a sick woman saw Rolle *"in habitu heremite
griseo ad eam venientem."* Allen notes that a late thirteenth–century manuscript has Pope
Celestine V appear *"avec sa robe grise, sa robe d'ermite, qu'il avait imposèe violemment aux
moines du Mont Cassin."* Apparently grey was the usual color for hermit's clothing,
occasionally with white. Cf. Allen, 526.

[8] Wooley (*Officium* 32,37) records the miracles; the temptation story is told by Rolle
in his *Commentary on the Canticles* (Corpus Christi College, Oxford MS. 193, f. 150^v) as
follows: *"Dum ego propositum singulare percepissem et, relicto habitu seculari, Deo pocius quam
homini deservire decrevissem, contigit quod quadam nocte in principio conversionis mee michi in
stratu meo quiescenti apparuit quedam iuvencula valde pulcra, quam ante videram et que me in*

cell from the torments of devils during her last hours. And there are other such cases mentioned.

After leaving the Daltons - -the exact timing of events is not clear - -Rolle presumably moved about the north country, living *"in Comitatu Richmundie"* and at Hampole. It appears from the *Melos Amoris* that the reasons for his movements may have been some disagreement with his patrons and a feud with the landed monks of Yorkshire which resulted from his attitude toward high living in religious communities. The *Incendium Amoris* tells of a period of persecution by those who had been Rolle's friends, but no details are forthcoming. At any rate, the movement of his cell from place to place was certainly in keeping with the volatile and individualistic personality which informs most of his writings. Finally, however, he settled in the rough, wooded country near Hampole priory where he died in the year 1349.

His Works

Although at present it is not possible to arrange Rolle's works in chronological order, they seem to have spanned the years from his early retirement into solitude to his death. He composed, both in Latin and English, works all of a religious nature but of several different kinds: meditations, scriptural commentaries, treatises on the spiritual life, particularly with relation to its mystical aspects, a "manual" of advice to pastors and their parishioners, a long poem of praise to the Virgin, epigrams, and even some lyrics. They were popular works, owned and read by wealthy laymen and ranking ecclesiastics, including those of the very monastic houses whose *delitie terrene* he had condemned. In addition, he must have been known on the Continent; there were a number of manuscripts in Sweden, Germany, and especially in those places that trace the route from England to Italy: Eâle, Metz, Trier, Brussels, and Ghent.

---

bono amore non modicum diligebat." The apparition was proved to be diabolic when it vanished at the words: *"O Ihesu, quam preciosus est sanguis tuus."* Cf. Allen 75, 466 – 470.

Although Rolle seems to have found preaching and the mystical life at odds, he never lost sight of the relation between his experience and that of his fellow Christians. H. E. Allen reminds us of the passages in the *Officium* which refer to his *"sanctis exhortationibus quibus quam plurimos convertit ad Deum"* (Wooley 32) and to the fact that *"ex habundantia caritatis sue, sollicitus erat se intimum familiarem exhibere reclusis et hiis qui spirituali indigebant consolatione"* (37). We have mentioned the *"verbum edificationis"* (32) he had for the lady of the Dalton house. With these intentions of edification, exhortation, and consolation, he wrote all his works, the English and the Latin. The longer, more substantial English treatises, *Ego Dormio, The Commandment,* and *The Form of Living,* were written in the form of epistles to nuns, and their acceptance may well have led him to adopt the vernacular for the *English Psalter* and the shorter prose pieces: "The Bee," " Desyre and Delit," " Gastly Gladnesse," " Seven Gifts of the Holy Spirit," " On the Ten Commandments," " Meditations on the Passion," and the lyric poems (Allen 246). These English works show a developing sense of prose style that places Rolle among the masters of devotional literature in the medieval period even though his career was terminated in middle age by death.

Rolle's first writing was in Latin: in four of his works he describes himself as *"iuvenis"* and a hermit so one or more of these may have been written as early as his eighteenth year. On the other hand, the term *"iuvenis"* can cover a span of life nearly twice eighteen years; again we must repeat that only critical analysis of the works themselves can be the basis of accurate chronology. The *Canticum Amoris,* the first of these works we have mentioned, is a poem in thirty – eight four – line stanzas, rhyming aaaa, in praise of the Virgin. It is in the manner of the secular love songs of the period, emphasizing her physical charms in "crude and extravagant" terms (Allen 90). The *Judica Me Deus* is actually four works loosely connected: the first is an answer to those who would censure him for moving his retreat to another location; the last three comprise a manual for parish priests taken often verbatim from the *Pars Oculi,* a well – known manual of the time. Throughout his life Rolle was concerned with the reform of the parish clergy, a concern which the Lollards seized upon to include him in the number of their apologists. Rolle in the *Judica* describes the virtues and vices of parish clergy, discusses the priest's function in the confessional, and provides a model sermon on the Last Judgment. Although it is not mentioned as one of the products of the "*iuvenis*," Allen considers the *Super Aliquos Versus Cantici Canticorum* as belonging to this stage in Rolle's literary development because the *Melos Amoris*, which is identified as such, seems on all the evidence to be a "more mature and forceful expression" of the ideas already stated in the *Cantici* (Arnould lxviii). She uses the *Cantici* as a touchstone for Rolle's characteristic style and content; it contains details of his mysticism and sidelong glances at his life, as do most of his writings. She describes it as a "diffuse and rambling exposition of the first five half–verses of the Song of Songs" (62).

The *Melos Amoris*, entitled with equal manuscript authority the *Melus Contemplativorum* and by Rolle himself "*de gloria et perfeccione sanctorum precellencium postillas*," is a very important and difficult work (Arnould xvi, Horstman II, xxxvi, n. 4). It relates and defines the process of his elevation to mystical heights while it refutes and condemns his detractors, all within a structure that is altogether unlike that of any other work in the Rolle canon. The prose is highly ornate and rhythmic, alliteration and assonance playing against each other in varying combinations, as for example:

> *Deinceps despexi dulcedinem deceptoriam, fugiens*
> *fallacias et figuras funeris, ac ficcionem fugans ne figerer in*
> *fomento floris formosi qui ut fenum marescit et migrat a mundo*
> *in mare meroris* (Arnould Cap. XL, p. 124, l. 4).

> *O capud captivorum, calliditas tua te contrivit, qui cupiens*
> *Christum confundere quassatus es et confusus! Crepa, qui*
> *corruisti a claro contubernio et privatus es a potestate qua te*
> *putabas perpetuo principasse! O tiranne, tabesce in tenebris, qui*
> *tentorium tuum tetendisti ut Tutorem nostrum trucidares!* (XXIX,
> p. 87, l. 5).

He liked to build sections around a biblical text as a motif, piling the phrases
and sections upon one another repetitively as far as content in concerned but
extracting from them in a quite "euphuistic" manner the utmost in stylistic
variation (Arnould lvii–lxv, Schneider *passim*). This, of course, pushes the
range of his vocabulary to the limit; Arnould records that titles for the Deity
alone total more than one hundred (lx).

Certainly later than the *Melos Amoris*, because it refers to it, and more
than likely in response to its mixed reception, Rolle composed the *Super
Lectiones Job in Officio Mortuorum*. The former was so idiosyncratic in its
style and so subjective in its interpretation of Christian experience, referring
everything to the ultimate of mystical experience, that he may have
anticipated on his pen the heavy hand of the establishment. An any rate, the
Job is a restrained, often scholastic, disquisition on the "disciplinary side of
religion" (Allen 137 seq.) in order by concentrating on the progress of the
sinner to move the reader to penitence. The interest on reforming the clergy
seen in the *Judica* is repeated in the *Job*, and there may also be in the
opening lines, according to Allen, some reference to the political situation
surrounding the fall of Edward II (1326–1330), both possible instances of
his using contemporary events as a focus for motivating repentance.

Other works somewhat like the *Melos* but more restrained in tone and
shorter are the Latin treatises and the English epistles. The *Liber de Amore
Dei Contra Amatores Mundi* and the *Incendium Amoris* deal specifically with
details of Rolle's mysticism – –Chapter 15 of the *Incendium* is perhaps the
most familiar of all his writings because it relates "how he came to the fire of
love" – –a frequently quoted and anthologized passage – –and in them as
well we find his devotion to the Holy Name of Jesus and an appeal for
friendship and for understanding of his mystical "*canor*." He also tries to
analyze he experience of "*canor*" and discusses "*calor*" and "*dulcor*." The
Incendium, however, deals with more than mystical experience: it defends the
hermit's life of retirement and discusses the contemplative life as the height
of spiritual endeavor. We find all the many facets of Rolle's writing:

theological argument, scriptural interpretation, direct exhortation, alliterative passages reminiscent of the *Melos*, and hints of autobiography.

The *Emendatio Vitae* is not as specifically mystical nor biographical but it too was very popular because of its tight structure and clear statement of the intent behind all Rolle's writing. This is achieved partly by including significant passages from other works, particularly from the *Contra Amatores Mundi*. The *Emendatio* mentions for the first time the three grades of love, namely the "inseparable," the "insuperable," and the "singular,"[9] which link it with the English epistles. Rolle modified the meanings of the terms which he derived from Richard of St. Victor possibly because of his reading of Gregory's *Homily on Ezechiel*[10] and of Bonaventura's *De Profectu Religiosorum*.[11]

The English epistles appear to be later than the treatises, except possibly for the *Emendatio*, because they show the terminology of an analyzed mysticism and their author's tempered individuality. They were surely written, as marginalia in several of the manuscripts testify, to religious women as from their spiritual advisor; as would be proper for a "ghostly father," they contain only oblique references to Rolle's personal experiences although the stamp of his life–long convictions is never absent. The *Ego Dormio* gives a complete account of his mysticism to a woman who is probably contemplating a life of solitude. Its quiet manner is enriched with poetical prose, inserted lyrics (for devotional purposes), rhyme and alliteration, and even ten lines of alliterative, unrhymed verse.

The Commandment deals less with the ecstatic life than with the purgative; it was apparently written for the beginner in convent life. There is no reason to doubt that it was intended for "*cuidam sorori de Hampole*" as

[9] Allen (201) notes that Rolle may have derived these terms from Richard of St. Victor's tract *De IV gradibus violentiae charitatis* (*PL*, CXCVI, 1207 seq.).

[10] Cf. II, v. (*PL*, LXXVI, 989).

[11] Cf. *De pro. rel.* II, xxv. This source was pointed out by A. Hahn, *Quellenuntersuchungen zu Richard Rolles englischen Schriften* (Berlin, 1900), pp. 7–8.

one very dependable manuscript testifies (Allen 255). The nun belonged to a house given to wearing secular finery; he reminds her that the babe in swaddling clothes cannot be found by such nuns.

The Form of Living is, based on the evidence, a rule written for Rolle's disciple, Margaret Kirkeby, presumably on her leaving the convent for the life of a recluse.   It is full of all his greatest concerns: an anatomy of mysticism, devotion to the Holy Name, the three levels of love and the sensual elements of mystical joy, many categorized pieces of advice drawn from the Fathers, and echoes of many of his own works (Allen 265).   The style is most sensitive and mature; alliteration and rhyme are used; two lyrics are inserted but integrated with the content.   It was an extremely popular work, existing in many manuscripts and later translated into Latin and into English verse.   Allen (268) ascribes *The Form of Living*, because it, like the *Emendatio*, *Ego Dormio*, and *Commandment*, are the only works that treat of the three stages of love, to the last years of his life.

The scriptural commentaries cannot be dated but it is possible that they were written throughout his life as a hermit.   Rolle was committed early to the study of the Bible, quoted it from intimate knowledge, worked it into his prose both as quotation and allusive phraseology, and used it to reflect his own moods and mystically centered concept of the good Christian life.   His methods range from the standard textbook approach of the *Psalters* to the long comment on a few short verses of the *Cantici*.   The shorter commentaries, however, demonstrate the same characteristic style of the self–confident writer who refers the biblical text to his own feelings and experiences, as much to interest the reader in the Bible itself and to teach him or minister to his needs.   The *Super Symbolum Apostolorum* and the *Super Orationem Dominicam* are more "scholarly" than the *Super Threnos*, *Super Apocalypsim*, or *Super Mulierem Fortem* but they do suggest their relation to the "ardent lovers of God" and to the "glory and perfection of the saints."   The latter three works are quite characteristic of Rolle in that despite their brevity they contain many of his usual preoccupations.

The *English* and *Latin Psalters* are largely independent of each other and intended for different audiences. The less educated reader of the vernacular could not be expected to deal with the four–fold sense of Scripture so the more complicated exegesis was reserved for the Latin work. Yet Rolle injects into each the fervor of his spirit. Dorothy Everett has shown that The *English Psalter* depends on the catena of Peter Lombard[12] and may derive some influence through the *Surtees Psalter*, an earlier metrical version, from the *Old English Glosses* (Everett, Part II), but nevertheless Allen points out that Rolle's "whole mystical doctrine could be expounded from his Psalters" (178).

Because of the great difference in method and intention, there is not much connection between the *Psalters* and the *Tractatus Super Psalmum Vicesimum* except that the *Latin Psalter* adopts the tropological interpretation. This may indicate Rolle's awareness of the fact that the tropological sense as applied to Psalm XX is quite rare.

Several commentaries grew out of Rolle's love of the Psalter.[13] Rolle wrote two expositions of the *Magnificat*; the English version is found with the *English Psalter* but the Latin version never with the *Latin Psalter*. The former describes the historical relation of the prayer to the life of the Virgin, while the latter provides a tropological exegesis of the prayer in relation to the individual human soul. The Latin *Super Magnificat*, however, is certainly by Rolle and could well be included with its corresponding Psalter: it records the writer's often attested devotion to the Holy Name and contains rhyme and alliteration.

---

[12] Discovered by H. Middendorff, *Studien über Richard Rolle von Hampole unter besonder Berücksichtigung seiner Psalmen – Commentare* (Magdeburg, 1888).

[13] The *De Dei Misericordia*, once thought to have been written by Rolle but now ascribed to John Waldeby (Hackett 464–66), is an allegory based on Psalm LXXXVIII. Not a very satisfying work when viewed from the vantage of Rolle's style, it is a standard medieval compilation of quotations from authorities – – Vincent of Beauvais, St. Anselm, St. Augustine, St. Bernard, Aristotle, St. Ambrose, Ovid, Seneca, and Vegetius – –held together by a loose allegorical framework.

Interest in Rolle and his writings was intense during the late Fourteenth Century and it continued so up to the Seventeenth; so many of Rolle's contemporaries read his works that Walter Hilton and the author of the *Cloud of Unknowing* felt compelled to caution Englishmen against the real psychological problems that could come of taking Rolle's program too literally. His mysticism was the major stimulus to interest in his works at that time, despite some minor use of his *English Psalter* by the Wycliffites adapted as it was by them to further their attacks on Church abuses, and it continued to be the motive for most of the work relating to him. After his death, the Reformation movement directed against the Lollards in the Fifteenth Century found his writings being utilized by the Cathedral chapters and particularly by the Carthusian monks of Syon and Shene monasteries.

During the period of the Church–wide Reformation of the Sixteenth Century, the "Feast of the Holy Name of Jesus," which had been included in the calendars of York and Sarum among many others because of the devotion to the Holy Name inspired by Rolle, was taken into the calendar of the Church of England where it has lasted until modern times. But the Counter–Reformation and printing combined to give Rolle his era of greatest influence; because of widespread interest in personal sanctity and in mysticism brought on by a general awareness of the deteriorating spiritual life in the Church many editions of Rolle's writings, including the one in which the *Tractatus* appears, were published in England and especially on the Continent up to the end of the Sixteenth Century.

The end of the Counter–Reformation also marked the end of interest in Rolle until the edition of Horstman in 1895, prompted no doubt by the resurgence of interest in mysticism, began the revival of Rolle study. In a sense, some work was wasted in commenting on the *Prick of Conscience*, once thought to be Rolle's, but the brilliant *Writings Ascribed to Richard Rolle*, published by Hope Emily Allen in 1927, provided a sound basis for further scholarship by identifying and relating manuscripts, texts, and biographical material in a complete and, for the time, exhaustive manner.

The Text

For his exegesis of Psalm XX, Rolle takes as his point of view the tropological, i.e., moral, sense of scriptural interpretation, as opposed to the allegorical interpretations of Augustine, Jerome, Peter Lombard, and others which see the psalm as prefiguring Christ. He explains the relation of the psalm to the individual soul in the usual way, that is, verse by verse, but the unmistakable stamp of his personality appears in his characteristic attitude toward what constitutes the motivation of the good Christian life, i.e., a burning love for Jesus, in the examples he chooses to exemplify the moral and the immoral man, and in the selection of a psalm which combines a song of praise of the king with a prayer for the punishment of his wealthy enemies – – the same alternation we discover in several other works by Rolle in which he condemns his adversaries while explaining a mystical transport.[14] We find, in addition to his attitude toward the process of biblical exposition, occasional personal, if rhetorically constructed, invocations to Christ and warnings to the reader as if his temperament were so caught up in the song of praise that the mystic cries out through the mouth of the exegete.

---

[14] For example, in the *Melos Amoris* (Corpus Christi College, Oxford MS. 193, f. 234^V), Rolle describes how his enemies continued to act after he has achieved ecstacy: "*Insurrexerunt in me iniqui ambulantes in eterno amore, et tribulantes temptaverunt, ut non tenear nisi trutannus, et deicerer a domibus in quibus diligebar.*" Shortly after this (f. 236) he says: "*Hic arguo contra aliquos procaciter errantes, qui forte ex invidia indigne dicebant. Asserebant etenim, sophistice loquentes, quod pro sumpto cibario sustinui sedere, et potibus deputantes quod piisimus prestavit, ac populis ut placeam plerique paventes publice predicabant penetentiam me pati; quod solummodo subegi subsidio celesti. Per ventrem repletum habere estimabant sessionem; in nocte suscept silenter et vigilans in gaudio, carpsi clamore[m] cordis constanter in impetu amoris, in canticum prorumpens, in laude canora liquide letabar.*" In the *Incendium Amoris* (Deanesly 170), Rolle suggests his past difficulties: "*Multi namque qui mecum loquebantur, similes fuerunt scorpionibus . . . a quorum labiis iniquis dolosis liberabit Deus animam meam.*" Allen discusses the autobiographical hints about Rolle's persecutions in *Writings* (470 seq.) and in the sections on *Office, Incendium, Melum,* and *Judica* (q.v.).

But this is more than exegesis: since tropology shows us what we must do, it is inevitable that the techniques of the preacher be added to those of the expositor. Rolle intends to move us as well as teach us so, just as the psalm moves from glory to punishment to praise, his commentary moves by successive emotive contrasts between his transports at the perception of Christ's glory and his sorrow, amply reinforced by biblical quotation and allusion, for those who would turn away from the love of Christ. As the *Melos Amoris* differs from and is yet related to the *Job*, the *Tractatus Super Psalmum Vicesimum* alternates between love and penitence and relates them. This is more than exegesis because there is more going on than the application of moral precepts to the human situation; Rolle subjectivizes and personalizes them. Since the structure of the psalm reflects his own individual *weltanschauung*, his choice of Psalm XX would seem a significant and an excellent one.

The *Tractatus Super Psalmum Vicesimum* begins with a brief prologue to induce in the reader a sense of his own inadequacy and of his dependence on the mercy of God because of which he may hope to profit from the words of the psalm.[15] The psalm encourages him to rejoice with the king; but who is the king? Rolle makes the necessary distinctions: the king can be either rich or poor, in the normal sense of the words, because it is only the just man who will rejoice with the angels; God pays no attention to wealth or position. Indeed, the rich man finds it more difficult to attain joy because he has more

---

[15] In the prologue Rolle applies his exposition to Englishmen, *"insula maris magni genitos et nutritos a faucibus maledicti draconis liberatos sapientie creatricis dulcedine,"* and so brings up a most interesting and complex piece of traditional, but seldom formulated, theology. *"Sapientie creatricis"* signifies the *sapientia increata* of God, a concept which has come down in both the Greek and the Hebraic traditions as "an attempt to bridge the gap between the complete transcendence of God and his immanence." This figure of divine wisdom is felt, rather than known, usually as a woman; in theology alone are Christ the masculine Logos and the feminine creating but increated wisdom equated. The tradition is long and inchoate, lasting well into the Seventeenth Century; witness the "Shee" in John Donne's *Anniversaries*. For an analysis of the question with sources, see Manley 20–40.

to renounce and farther to fall. So let the sinner beware! And since the just man will rejoice with the King of Heaven, he is a king himself.

What is his kingdom? The just man rules over the world and his flesh, the inclinations to evil within him, and his subjects are his thoughts. When he has achieved mastery, says Rolle, he rules over four kingdoms:

> *regnum mundi per paupertatem voluntariam, regnum carnis per temperativam prudentiam, regnum diaboli per humilem patientiam, regnum celi per charitatem perfectam.*

In the strength of the Lord he wins glory and "upholds his people," and so he may rejoice exceedingly. The author makes it unmistakably clear that the king's objective is the love of Jesus Christ: "*qui Christum amare negligit, in illo penitus gaudere nescit.*" This love is offered by Christ, however, not only as the eventual reward in the next life but also as the incentive to virtuous action in this. Foreseeing our difficulty, Christ gives us a taste of future glory so that we may be motivated to receive its fullness.

As we progress, it becomes increasingly more evident that Rolle is thinking of the rise of man from his renunciation of sin to his glory in heaven in terms of the mystic's way from purgation and illumination to contemplation. This is not defined with any of the precise terminology we find in other works by Rolle that deal explicitly with his mysticism, but the diction and phraseology seem to indicate much more than rhetorical *amplificatio.* As his heart's desire the king is granted: "*veri luminis claritatem, audiri melos angelicum, videre incircumscriptum lumen eterni amoris, delitiarum canticum canere mellifluum.*" The normal business of everyday life is no longer acceptable to the king so, "*igne Spiritus Sancti calefactus eternitatisque amore liquescens, totum cor fervor dulcifluus obumbrat.*" He is "*ad summa elevatur,*" and the way in which this elevation is expressed certainly suggests the "*calor, dulcor, canor*" of the mystical ecstasy of the *Melos Amoris* and the *Incendium.* The various words for "sweetness" occur very many times throughout the treatise, associated with praise, joy, and the purification from sin.

The crown of the soldier–king is the crown of joy with Christ as its precious stone; this is the one point which Rolle allegorizes within his basically moral interpretation. Père de Lubac reminds us that tropology and allegory were always closely connected--when they were not the same thing: what Christ offers us of Himself and what we must do for Him are both actually represented in the reward of our striving.[16] The "*lapis pretiosus*" theme is carried to a great rhetorical crescendo until the author *in propria persona* exclaims:

> *O lapidem pretiosum, super aurum et omnem mundi dulcedinem desidero illum!*

The eternal possession of the crown suggests to Rolle its opposite so he contrasts the glory of heaven with the expectation of the wicked after death. But he cannot dwell for long on the dreariness of damnation; it is effective as contrast but his genius is of a different order. He cannot resist punctuating the torments of the damned with a personal invocation: "*Veni, dulcedo suavissima! Veni, dilecte mi!*" But a proper appreciation of the next verse ("*Magna est gloria eius in salutari tuo*") requires the strong reminder that glory cannot be achieved without penitence. Even infants dying without Baptism are not spared and those living out their lives must take advantage of the time that the mercy of God has provided them. The strong king, however, can ignore worldly vanities, earn the love of Christ, and then will not be able to feel the worst that the world can offer. In a return to one of his favorite

---

[16] Henri de Lubac (Part I, Vol. 2, 544) says that there is a "*double tropologie. En les distinguant l'une et l'autre, Honorius dit que l'une conjoint l'âme à l'esprit, pour que de leur union résulte le 'bonum opus,' et que l'autre nous unit au Christ par la charité.*" The statement he refers to is from Honorius, *In Cant.*: "*Juxta tropologiam etiam fiunt nuptiae duobus modis: uno quo anima Christo per dilectionem copulatur; alio quo anima, quod est inferior vis interioris hominis spiritui, qui est superior ejus, per consensum divinae legis conjungitur, de quo conjungio spiritualis proles, id est bonum opus gignitur*" (*PL*, CLXXII, 349 BC). The mystical thrust behind Rolle's entire commentary would seem to bear out both aspects of such a double tropology.

texts, Rolle quotes such a king as saying: "*Amore langueo*," because he has reached salvation.

The ecstasy of the *Canticle* attendant upon the allegorical marriage of Christ and Ecclesia reminds the hermit of his solitude; the role of the contemplative is now eulogized and his special ability to be actually taken up from the problems of existence to a glimpse of the joys to come. The contemplative, i.e., the one most in love with Christ, always for Rolle the norm against which religious perfection is judged, seems to function here as a type of the good Christian:

> *Non mireris igitur, si gaudent qui divino amori eligitur et*
> *supernorum iubilo contemplativus esse inspiratur.... Iste nimirum*
> *est rex de quo adhuc propheta loqui non trepidat....*

This is the man who will not be moved if he hopes in the Lord; and the idea of movement is particularly significant for Rolle at this juncture. In the tropological sense, of course, the man who trusts in God's mercy and loves Christ will not be "moved" in the sense of "being shaken" from joy by sin and hardship; this is conventional enough. But Rolle, whose normal posture for contemplation we know was sitting, gives us here a pleasant and effective metaphorical passage on the virtues of quiet sitting.[17]

---

[17] Rolle heartily endorses sitting for the contemplative; he returns to it repeatedly in his works and the only picture we have of him, in British Museum MS. Cotton Faustina B vi. Pt. II, f. 8b, shows him in this position. For the comments of his enemies about his sitting, see note 12. His own ideas are reflected in the following: "*Sanctus solitarius, quia pro Salvatore suo sedere sustinuit in solitudine, sedem in celestibus accipiet auream et excellentem inter ordines angelorum*" (*Melos* 146,2). "*Siquidem si oracionem contra hostes offerens Omnipotenti, meditacionemque mellifluam in memoria retinens et ruminans, non pro modico mobilis quemadmodum stulti qui non stabiliuntur, sed sollicitus infatigabiliter sederit, procul dubio divinam dulcedinem amplius habebit*" (35, 8). "*Et nota nimirum . . . ut umbra se operiat alarum Amati, sedere, not stare vel ire aut currere, commemoratur . . .*" (127,4).

In *The Form Of Living* (47) Rolle writes: "In whatever state it be that men are in the greatest rest of body and soul, and least occupied with any needs or business of this world [in

The man who runs cannot fix his gaze on any object very steadily or very long, for he is "too much moved." Walking is better, but also short–lived; standing better yet, but fatigue must eventually cause one to waver. If God is the object of the soul and if movement shows a lack of moral resolve, then the "*amator Christi*" can contemplate his beloved best and for the longest time if he sits. "*Nimirum perpauci ad hanc pertingunt*," but this is what the perfect lover of Christ metaphorically, and the mystics actually, will do; and the more perfect the less moved. If the "king" is equated with the mystic, or even with the Christian who has achieved a high degree of love for Christ, the next step is to those who have not moved in the direction of love for Christ. Those who "run" or "walk" deserve, more often

---

that state they may most love God]. For the thought of the love of Jesus Christ and of the joy that lasts forever, seeks rest without, that it be not hindered by comers and goers and occupation with worldly things. And it seeks within a great silence form the noise of covetings and of vanities and of earthly thoughts. And all those especially that love contemplative life seek rest in body and soul. For a great doctor says that they are God's throne who dwell still in one state and are not running about, but are established in the sweetness of God's love.

And I have loved to sit, not for penance, nor for fancy that I have wished men to speak of me, nor for any such thing: but only because I loved God more, and the comfort of love lasted longer with me than when going or standing or kneeling. For sitting I am most in rest and my heart is most upward. But peradventure it is not therefore best for another to sit, as I did and will do till my death, unless he were disposed as I am, in his soul.

The *Incendium Amoris* (184–5) records another echo of our commentary: "*Porro, ut potui in scripturis perscrutari, inveni et cognovi quidem quod summus amor Christi in tribus consistit: in* fervore, *in* canore, *et in* dulcore; *et hec tria ego expertus sum in mente non posse diu persistere sine magna quiete. Ut si velim stando vel ambulando contemplari, vel procumbendo, videbam me multum ab illis deficere, et quasi desolatum me existimare. Unde hac necessitate compulsus ut in summa devocione quam habere possem et perseverare, sedere elegi. Huius rei causa non ignoro quia si homo multum stet vel ambulet corpus eius fatigatur et sic impeditur anima et quodammodo lacescit pre onere. Et non est in sua summa quiete, et per consequens nec in perfeccione, quia secundum philosophum, sedendo et quiescendo fit anima prudens. Qui ergo adhuc magis stando quam sedendo in divinis delectatur, sciat se a contemplacionis culmine longe distare.*"

than not, the justice of God. Rolle accordingly reminds us of what they will lose if they do not repent and reject the things of this world.

Rolle tends to follow the traditional lines more closely in the second part of the psalm. Verses 9–13 do not seem to affect him as strongly as the verses of exaltation although they do evidence his usual attitude toward the enemies of Christ: they are too attached to their own pleasure in worldly possessions. In other words, he sees sin as essentially a perversion of the love they should have for Christ rather than as a juridical relationship. His treatment of these verses is far from sketchy, and his tone is more that of compassion and regret than of condemnation. His lines are thicker with biblical quotation and more conventional in approach than the prior two–thirds of the treatise; the effectiveness of this section is due rather to careful selection (even the word "selection" must be offset by the awareness that Rolle knew the Psalter and other large portions of the Bible intimately) of resonant quotations than to essentially original composition.

Rolle closes by recalling the opening words of the psalm with their note of joy and, having quoted the Psalmist's parting invocation, adds a formal prayer of his own which stresses again the glory in heaven awaiting the lovers of Christ. We should not think of the conclusion as pure formality or as some topos of the commentary form. A reader of the *Melos* or the *Incendium* could not think of singing and praising God as a ritualistic thing for Rolle. Behind all of his writings we feel the mind and heart of the hermit reaching out to the reader from the abundance of his love for Christ, to those in need of spiritual exhortation and consolation. The existential relation is never absent: all of life is conceived in terms of one's attachment to Christ being put into practice by as humble an action as sitting down or as exalted an act as seeing God face to face. The tree stump on which Rolle has been pictured makes a fitting symbol for the central focus of the *Tractatus*, as well as all of Rolle's writings: the quiet love of Christ and for Christ leads to glory.

The commentary tradition behind the *Tractatus* by the hermit of Hampole, insofar as it has been published and therefore been accessible to this editor, proves how much Rolle's work is the product of an imaginative and forceful personality. Because of his experiences at Oxford with scholasticism and in Yorkshire with the wealthy monastic orders, and chiefly because of the point of view derived from his mystical experiences, Rolle brings to his treatise on the Twentieth Psalm an insight into the problems of his time (and of any time) that is fresh, creative, and finely controlled. Seen against this tradition and his own conventional *Latin* and *English Psalters*, the *Tractatus* truly becomes, as the Cologne, 1536 edition puts it, a "*tractatus quidem peculiaris.*" Of all the psalms, Rolle selected only Psalm XX for an individual treatise, the analysis of which shows that it is as much a vehicle for expressing his own thoughts and feelings by means of the psalm as it is an exposition of the meaning of the psalm itself. Significantly, nowhere else in the tradition to my knowledge does there exist a treatment of Psalm XX separated as Rolle's is from its Psalter context.

The tradition, except for one commentary by Thomas de Jorz, is solidly allegorical in its method, linking, often explicitly, the opening of Psalm XX to the last verse of Psalm XIX: "*Domine, salvum fac regem.*"[18] Augustine in the *Enarratio in Psalmos* says: "*Titulus notus est; de Christo canitur.*" St.

---

[18]   The following are all the published commentaries that deal with Psalm XX arranged in chronological order according to the date of the commentator's death: Augustine, *Enar. in Psal., CCSL*, XXXVIII, 115; Jerome, *Comm. in Psal., CCSL*, LXXII, 197; Arnobius Junior, *Comm. in Psal., PL*, LIII, 551–2; Cassiodorus, *Exp. Psal., CCSL*, XCVII, 181; Remi d'Auxerre, *Enar. in Psal., PL*, CXXXI, 245–9; Bruno Herbipolensis, *Exp. Psal., PL*, CXLII, 104–6; Bruno, *Exp. in Psal., PL*, CLII, 715–18; Manegold, *In Psal. lib. Exeg., PL*, XCIII, 587; Anselm of Laon, *Comm. in Psal., PL*, CXVI, 259–62 and *Glossa Ordinaria, PL*, CXIII, 872–3; Odon d'Asti, *Exp. in Psal., PL*, CLXV, 1190–2; Bruno d'Asti, *Exp. in Psal., PL*, CLXIV, 762–4; Peter Lombard, *Comm. in Psal., PL*, CXCI, 219–25; Gerhoch, *Comm. in Psal., PL*, CXCIII, 975–88; Bonaventura, "Exp. in Psal.," *Opera Omnia* (Paris, 1867), IX, 179–80; Albertus Magnus, "Comm. in Psal.," *Opera Omnia* (Paris, 1892), XV, 285–95; and Thomas de Jorz, *Comm. super Psal.* (Venice, 1611), 232 seq. The great collector of commentaries and commentator himself, Cornelius a Lapide, in his *Commentarii in Scripturam Sacram* (London, 1864), VII, 60–62, shows that the main line of allegorical interpretation continued into the Seventeenth Century. Those commentaries still in manuscript may be found in Spicq (396).

Jerome, commenting on the first verse in his *Commentarioli in Psalmos,* says: *"Iste est rex, (cui, ut in superiori psalmo scribitur, secundum formam serui oratur salus): Xpistus 'rex regum et dominus dominantium.'"* Cassiodorus in his *Expositio Psalmorum* has the most complete discussion of the relation:

> *In finem psalmus David. Ideo titulus hic nono decimo psalmo par est, quoniam et iste de Domino quidem Salvatore sed sub aliqua diuersitate dicturus est. Superior namque continet orationem prophetae, et confidentiam qua liberandus est a cladibus huius saeculi populus christianus. Nunc quidam panegyricus de incarnatione ipsius dicitur, et postea deitatis eius facta narrantur: ut omnes intelligant eumdem esse Mariae semper Virginis Filium, quod Patris Verbum. Duas enim naturas in Christo Domino salutariter credimus, deitatis et humanitatis, quae in unam personam per infinita saecula incommutabiliter perseuerant. Quod ideo frequenter repetendum est, quia uitaliter et auditur semper et creditur.*

Cassiodorus goes on to divide the psalm into three sections:

> *In prima narratione psalmi huius, uerba prophetae sunt ad Deum Patrem de incarnatione dominica. Secunda diversas uirtutes eius gloriamque describit; declarans a parte qua passus ad quam summam rerum apicemque ipso largiente perueniret. Tertia idem propheta conuertitur ad Dominum Christum, ubi more desiderantium optat illa in iudicio eius fieri quae nouit esse uentura* (181).

In general, the tradition agrees with this arrangement although a number of writers combine the first two parts into one. A complete explication of all the minor variations in the allegorical interpretation of Psalm XX would be out of place here because the works involved are readily available, but a résumé of the main points would serve to indicate the main line of the tradition which Rolle it appears both assumed and ignored.

First, the psalm is of Christ the King who will rejoice that by the power of the Father He is able to save men from their sins. The Father granted Him His wish to eat the Pasch, to lay down His life, and to take it up again, so that all might be fulfilled through Him. The Father, because of the blessing He had given His Son, i.e., freedom from sin, placed upon Him the crown of the Church with the apostles as its precious stones so that all men might be glorified through Him. The Son in His human nature asked for resurrection from the dead and for eternal life and He was granted it and the Church with Him.

In the second part, we are told that glory and great beauty will be bestowed on Christ the Saviour when He returns to the right hand of the Father – –"*gloriam de iudicio, decorem de maiestate.*" The Psalmist, according to Augustine and Jerome, declares that the "*benedictio*" for Christ is the "*gaudium cum vultu tuo*" of the second part of the verse. Many interpreters, Cassiodorus perhaps the first among them, feel that this is predicated of the members of the Church who will rise with Christ, but all are agreed that eventual joy is a result of the Incarnation and the Resurrection signified by the psalm. Verse 8 allegorized says that Christ the King trusted in the Father because of the humility and obedience proper to the Son's human nature "*usque ad mortem crucis,*" and because He received mercy, He was not shaken from His resolve.

With verse 9, the Psalmist begins the third (or second) section on the power of Christ shown at the Judgment. Some commentators feel that those judged are the Jews who failed to see Christ's majesty under His humility, others that these are simply the souls who hated Him and sinned. But whoever is meant, the fires of their consciences will burn them, and God the Son will confine them in hell. There is some disagreement about what is meant by the phrase "*reliquiis tuis*"; it is suggested by some that it refers to Enoch and Elias who have been left to prepare the elect for the face – to – face meeting with Christ. Perhaps it is just the elect. But all agree that finally we can sing the King's praise by deeds as well as words.

It is in this last section of the psalm that the allegorical method tends to become indistinguishable from the tropological – – except for the focus on Christ as the Judge provided by the preceding verses.   The immediate application of the action of Christ as Judge to the human situation is so hard to resist that the tendency is to obscure the relation between Judgment and the two natures of Christ, His power and majesty, and His final vindication, i.e., the allegorical relation.   Any given psalm, of course, could require to be read in one sense up to a certain point and in another sense beyond it, and many writers are not concerned to keep the various senses apart.   A brief look at the historical development of tropology as one of the exegetical senses, however, should enable us to distinguish it from, and relate it to, allegory.

Augustine's *De Doctrina Christiana* speaks only of a literal and a spiritual sense of scriptural interpretation, all of the allegorical, typological, moral, and anagogical senses, as we have come to know them, being contained in the latter.[19]   For many writers this was the only distinction, though their terms might be different, but Gregory in particular favored a specifically moral sense:

> *Sensus ergo allegorical sub brevitate transcurrimus, ut ad moralitatis latitudinem citius venire valeamus.* . . .

> *Haec nos, fratres carissimi, pro indagandis allegoriae mysteriis succincte transcurrisse sufficiat; nunc ad intuendam latius rei gestae moralitatem animus recurrat.*[20]

---

[19] *PL*, XXXIV, 15–122; see especially Book III.

[20] Greg., *In ev.*, h. 40, n. 2–3 (*PL*, LXXVI, 1302 AB, 1304 C) as quoted in de Lubac (551). Most of the ideas on the history and development of tropology contained in this discussion are directly derived from this most excellent study by Père Henri de Lubac. The level of generalization intended in this introduction cannot, of course, do justice to all the complexities of the tradition behind fourteenth–century exegesis; for this the reader is referred to Père de Lubac's work and to the older and somewhat superficial volume of Spicq.

His moralizing was literally a wandering off from an allegorical point along some moral path that attracted him at the moment.[21] It was the Victorines who in the Twelfth Century carefully distinguished the knowledge of meaning ("*cognitio veritatis*") from the example of proper action ("*forma virtutis*"). Basically, the word "tropology" derived from "trope" or "figure of speech" (*sermo conversivus*) and thus could designate any meaning beyond the literal. Gradually, chiefly because of St. Paul, allegory became associated with foreshadowing the relation of the Old Testament to Christ in the New Testament in His dealings with His Church on earth; the mystical interpretation of the relation of Christ and His Spouse the Church in the next life fell to anagogy; and so the moral exposition was left to tropology.

What had been for Peter Comestor the "*sermo conversivus pertinens ad mores animi*" was altered by the Victorines.[22] As de Lubac explains it:

> *A la suite d'Hughes de Saint–Victor, Robert de Melun*
> *amplifiera:* "Tropologia idem sonat, quam sermo conversivus,
> eo quod factum tale designat, ad quod nos secundum moralis
> aedificationis institutionem necessarium est converti." *La*
> *logique de cet* "eo quod," *transposant la* "conversio" *du discours à*
> *la conversion morale, n'était pas très rigoureuse . . . . D'autres*
> *diront plus simplement, se portant tout de suite au terme:*
> "Tropologia est moralis sermo," *ou* "moralis scientia." *On écrira*
> *donc, comme si l'on avait oublié l'origine grammaticale du mot:*
> "Tropologia est moralis sermo . . . et fit apertis verbis, aut
> figuratis." *On le pouvait d'ailleurs, en forçant un peu une autre*
> *signification du mot, qui, appliqué non plus à la grammaire ou au*
> *style, mais à l"homme, équivalait à* "maniere d'être or d'agir,
> habitude, moeurs." *– –Mais il ne faut pas attacher trop*
> *d'importance à ces définitions nominales, qui n'entrent pas dans*
> *le vif de la réalité; elles servent du moins à distinguer un sens*
> *biblique d'un autre; tel ce type courant, que nous empruntons au*

---

[21] For a study of Gregory's method in more detail, see B. Smalley, 32–35.

[22] *PL*, CXCVIII, 1055 A.

Speculum *de l'Ecole de Saint – Victor:* "Allegoria dicitur,
quando per factum intelligitur aliud factum . . . Tropologia est,
quando per factum ostenditur aliud faciendum.*"*

*Autrement dit, la tropologie dont il est question dans
l'énumération des sens de l'Ecriture n'est pas le* "moralis sermo"
qui est prononcé "apertis verbis*"; il n'est pas cette* "simplex
moralitas*" qui découle immédiatement de l'* "historia*" lorsque
celle – ci propose de bons exemples ou fait détester les mauvais*
(552).

Père de Lubac does not allow us to oversimplify the terms by keeping
them apart; since they are meanings of the same Scriptures, they must also be
related.   And tropology itself is not just *"moralis sermo"* in *"figuratis verbis"*;
there is a double tropology (Cf. n. 14 supra), one natural, one mystical:

L'une "moralisee*" la donnée biblique, à la manière dont peut être
*"moralisee" une donnée quelconque de la littérature, de l'homme
et de l'univers; .... Mais l'autre tropologie, celle dont la place est
troisième dans la formule la plus frèquente et la plus logique du
quaduple sens, – – et que ne méconnaissent pas ceux mêmes qui
n'en font pas mention distincte, – –a rapport au sens spirituel
propre à l'Ecriture, non seulement en tout réalité, mais en toute
nécessité. Elle concourt à l'elaboration de ce sense qui caractérise
la seule Ecriture. Elle ne précède pas* "l'édifice spirituel,*" mais elle
*"s'y ajoute," ou plutôt elle s'y déploie, pour le compléter. Elle est
au dedans de l'allégorie. Elle fait pertie intégrante du mystère.
Venant après l'aspect objectif qu'en est l'allégorie, elle en
constitue l'aspect subjectif. Elle en est, si l'on peut dire,
l'intussusception, l'intériorisation; elle nous l'approprie. C'est
dans ce* mysterium *que la tropologie puise ses exempla. Elle est
ce* "mysticus moralitatis sensus,*" cette* "spiritualis vitae
intelligentia,*" qu'un regard exercé discerne partout dans les deux
Testaments. Si l'allégorie, à partir des faits de l'histoire, envisage*

le corps mystique en sa tête, ou dans son ensemble, la tropologie
l'envisage en chacun de ses membres: ... (554 – 5).

Thomas de Jorz wrote his dual allegorical – tropological
interpretation – – the only tropological commentary other than Rolle's that I
have discovered – – in a verse – by – verse fashion, alternating the levels of
exegesis.[23] We find evidence of this *"spiritualis vitae intelligentia"* in his
combination of allegory and tropology. The "edifice" image recalls Peter
Comestor's remarks on the "senses" in his prologue to the *Historia
Scholastica*:

Holy Scripture is God's dining room, where the guests are
made soberly drunk ... History is the foundation ... allegory
the wall ... tropology the roof ....

---

[23] It may not have been de Jorz who wrote the *Commentarius super Psalmos*, Venice,
1611 but rather Thomas Walleys, as J. Echard believes. J. Quetif et J. Echard, *Scriptores
ordinis Praedicatorum*, Paris, I – II, 1719; ed. R. Coulon (Rome, 1910), 509: *"Item incepit
scribere super Psalterium, & morte praeventus non complevit.* Hactenus Valleoletanus.

*"Hoc scriptum super Psalmos F. Sixtus Lambertus sodalis noster Lucensis putavit se
invenisse, & hortante inquit magistro ordinis Augustino Galaminio postea cardinali reipsa edidit
sub hoc titulo:* Commentarius super Psalmos F. Thomae Jorgii Anglice ord. Praedic. S. R. E.
cardinali & episcopi Sabinensis. *Ubi erratum, legendum enim presbyteri tit. S. Sabinae, non
episcopi Sabinen. Venetiis, Evangelistae Deuchini 1611 fol. pp. 311 & 148.* Pr. Beatus qui
custodit verba prophetiae libri hujus. Apoc. 22 *Commentarius est in XXXVII priores Psalmos
seu duos promos nocturnos, ut tam loquebantur.*

*Dubium tamen mihi haud modicum est, an ille commentarius sit Thomae Jorzii, nam
Thomae Wallensi seu Guallensi hoc opus omnes notitiae datae videntur asserere. De isto
Laurentius Pignon dicit in duos nocturnos psalterii primos scripsisse. Codices Angli & Belgici
Wallensis nomen praefixum habent. Principium idem,* Beatus qui custodit &c. *indicatur. Sixtus
Senensis codicem MS Venetum SS. Jo. & Pauli laudans dicit praeferre nomen Thomae Anglici
patria Galensis, idem esse principium, revera addit esse tantum in XXV primos psalmos, sed forte
codicem non accurate evolverat. Videsis postea ad 1340 ubi de Thoma Wallensi: hic dubium
meum lectoribus proposuisse sufficiat."*

We notice at the beginning of his exposition of Psalm XX that he relates one sense to the other as solidly as would a skilled carpenter:

> *EXAUDIAT TE DOMINUS. Psal. Iste agit de Christo quantum ad ipsius duplicem dignitatem, scilicet, Pontificalem, & Regalem, & dividitur in duas partes, quia primo agit de Christo tanquam Sacerdote, & Pontifice. Secundo de ipso tanquam Rege, & Principe, ibi. In potentatibus. Sciendum est quod Psalm. in Psalm. isto texens prophetiam de Christo, proponit eam per modum orationis pro Christo, non quod intenderit aliquid impetrare pro seipso. Sperebat enim se fore membrum Christi, & ideo se participaturum bonis Christi. Alia causa est, quia circa ea quibus texit haec prophetia, non solum illustratur intellectus, sed etiam vehementer inflammatur affectus, & ideo per modum orationis suum exprimebat affectum; .... Sciendum est autem quod ea, quae in hoc Psalmo de Christo Pontifice intelliguntur, possunt convenire cuilibet fideli, vel Ecclesiam, & dupliciter exponi potest.*[24]

Here we see that he applies the meaning of the psalm to Christ, thus linking the two Testaments, and includes Christ's members to complete the structure.

In his exposition of the last verse of Psalm XIX, Thomas discusses the allegorical nature of the king in a long passage and then moves to the tropological; in explaining the latter he recalls a passage from Gregory that may also have caught Rolle's attention: Thomas writes,

> *. . . quod Rex debet esse de genere illorum, quibus principatur, sic & Christus, ut super vos regnaret congruentius, de genere nostro esse voluit. Act. 17 Ipsius enim & genus sumus. Ideo præceptum fuit Deut. 17. Non poteris alterius generis tibi Regem facere, qui non sit frater tuus. Vel Rex iste est ipsa mens, cuius anima*

---

[24] *PL*, CXCVIII, 1053 as quoted in Smalley, 242.

Regnum esse debet, cuius salus hoc patitur. Vel Rex est totus
homo qui bene se regit. Unde Greg. 26. moral. Super illud Job
36. *Reges in solio colocat, dicit sic. Sancti viri Reges vocantur,*
qui prœlati cunctis motibus carnis, modo luxuriœ appetitum
refrenant, modo estum avaritiœ temperant, modo gloriam
œlationis inclinant, cœt. Reges igitur sunt qui tentationem
suarum motibus non consentiendo succumbere, sed regendo
posse noverunt. Hœc ille. Subditi igitur istius sunt motus, &
passiones carnis (222 – 3).

The tropological part of this passage appears almost verbatim in his
exposition of Psalm XX, verse 7, the only verbal relation between his
treatments of the two psalms; in content, of course, the latter psalm picks up
the idea of the "king" from the last verse of the former as does the standard
allegorical line, but there is no stated reference back to Psalm XIX as the
commentary on Psalm XX begins.

Thomas de Jorz's exegetical technique is the same as that which
begins Psalm XX:

DOMINE IN VIRTUTE TUA &c. *Psal. Iste est de Christo Rege*
nostro, in quo psalm. duo facit, quia primo agit de ipsius lœtitia,
quam habet de beneficiis sibi, & suis prœstitis. Secundo de eius
potentia, quam ostendet in puniendo reprobos, ibi. Inveniatur,
&c. primo igitur tangit ipsius gaudium. Secundo ipsius meritum,
ibi, Quoniam Rex, &c. Primo tangit sui gaudii vehementiam.
Secundo illius gaudii materiam, ibi, Desiderium. Sciendum est
autem, quod iste versus potest exponi dupliciter: Vno modo de
Christo: Alio modo de quolibet electo (232).

The allegorical treatment is much as expected: the two psalms are linked
together and after verse eight of Psalm XX there is no distinction made
between levels. The moral interpretation assumes control as it were to "roof
the house" of the king, and the allegory fades away until it is vaguely recalled
by the last verse. It is a well constructed commentary, clear, authoritative,

and learned--even the Arabs are cited; but there is no personal touch at all. Thomas explains how the psalm applies to Christ and to the members of the Ecclesia, but not to himself; he gives all the possibilities of interpretation known to him from allegory and tropology, but he does not move us. He is thoroughly conventional.

The conclusion we draw is that the tropology of Thomas de Jorz, to quote Honorius again, is the ordinary kind that "*conjoint l'âme à l'esprit, pour que de leur union résulte le* 'bonum opus'" while that of Rolle "*nous unit au Christ par la charité*," partly because he moves us by the strength of his own enthusiasm, it is true, but partly because he holds out to us the certainty gained by experience that such union and such love is real and effective and sweet.[25] His originality consists in the energy and polish of a personal style and in the authority and the uniqueness of a point of view which cause his tropological exegesis to incandesce.

Citations of the Text

The *Tractatus Super Psalmum Vicesimum* was noted by Boston of Bury (c. 1410) as belonging to the library of his own house. As quoted by Allen (418) from Thomas Tanner, *Bibliotheca Britannico*–Hibernia (London, 1748), p. xxxviii, the entry reads as follows:

> *Ricardus, heremita de Ampole, floruit circa A. C. . . . et scripsit*
> Incendium amoris, lib. i. 82 [Boston's number for Bury library]
> *Melos amoris, lib. i. 82. De amore divino. 82. De timore Domini*
> *et contemptu mundi. 82. Vehiculum vitae sive xii capitula. 82.*
> *Super lectiones De officio mortuorum. 82. Super Psalmum,*
> *Domine in virtute. 82. Super Psalterium . . .in Latin. et Angl.*
> *Super Lamentationes Jeremiae. Super quartum librum*
> *Sententiarum: Pr. Secundum quosdam. De glorificatione*
> *sanctorum.*

---

[25] Cf. n. 14 *supra*.

The *Tractatus* is also noted by John Bale (c. 1548–51) in his *Index*, ed. R. L. Poole and M. Bateson (*Anecdota Oxoniensa*, 1902), pp. 348–52 as follows: (pp. 348–9) *Ex collegio Martonensi, Oxon.* (Cod. lxviII. f. 74b [Coxe, p. 42]) *Ricardus Remyngton, de Hampole, heremita scripsit,*

. . . .

In psalmum vicesimum, li. i. *"Cum Christus, qui est veritas, dicat."* (pp. 351–2) *Ex Ayloto Holte, Buriensi.*

. . . .

Super ps., Domine in virtute li. i. Bostonus.
Ricardus Hampole, heremita, vir eruditus, scripsit,

. . . .

In psalmum vicesimum, li. i. *"Cum Christus qui est veritas divina."*

Quotations from the *Tractatus* occur in Oxford Bodleian MSS. Ashmole 751, ff. 13^v, 61 (late Fourteenth Century) and in Hatton 97 (Summa Catalogue No. 4070), ff. 68–72 (early Fifteenth Century). A single quotation appears in British Museum MS. Roy 5 A. vi., ff. 13^v – 30^v (dated 1446, scribe John Celstan). Some quotations appear in a work, extant in five manuscripts, entitled *De Excellentia Contemplationis.*[26] This is a compilation of excerpts from several of Rolle's works that deal with aspects of mysticism but it is not known whether Rolle actually composed it himself. The reference in the *Officium* to events drawn *"ex scriptura manus proprie huius sancti reperta post mortem in uno libello de suis operibus compilato"*: suggests that Rolle compiled at least one such work, and four of the five manuscripts ascribe it to him; but the argument to support his authorship, particularly since the work is so clumsily constructed from the parts of such carefully composed treatises, is very far from convincing (Wooley 36).

---

[26] The five manuscripts are: B. Mus. Egerton 671, ff. 27–47^v, 15th Century; B. Mus. Add. 24661, ff. 49^v–58^v, 15th Century; Douay 396, ff. 193–196, 15th Century; Uppsala Univ. C. 17, ff. 167–182, 15th Century; and Uppsala Univ. C. 631, ff. 1–13, 15th Century. See Allen (320–23) for a discussion of the *De Excellentia Contemplationis*.

II

The Manuscripts

The text of the *Tractatus Super Psalmum Vicesimum* is witnessed by six manuscripts and one edition which was printed at Cologne in 1536. *Incipit:* *"Cum Christus qui est veritas . . . "* (except C which begins at *"Domine, in virtute tua . . ."*); *explicit: "gloriemur in seculo seculorum. Amen."* The description of manuscript Bodley 861 is based primarily on the treatment done by Hope Emily Allen. The description of all other manuscripts but Uppsala C. 621 are derived from my own analysis of the microfilms and from published catalogue descriptions. In some instances the dating in the catalogues may need some revision.

Oxford:

A.   **Bodley MS. 861 (B)** contains all the Latin works of Richard Rolle except the *Canticum Amoris, Super Mulierem Fortem,* and *De Misericordia.* In addition to works by others on ff. 133 – 137^v and on f. 142, the manuscript contains:

1.   *Latin Psalter* and *Canticles* (ff. 1 – 49)
2.   *Melos Amoris* (ff. 51 – 81)
3.   *Commentary on the Canticles* (ff. 81 – 90)
4.   *Tractatus Super Psalmum Vicesimum* (ff. 90 – 93)
5.   *Liber De Amore Dei Contra Amatores Mundi* (ff. 93 – 100^v)
6.   *Judica Me Deus,* A (ff. 100^v – 102^v)
7.   *Incendium amoris* (ff. 102^v – 122)
8.   *Super Apocalypsim* (ff. 123 – 128).
9.   *Regula Vivendi Distincta In Duodecim Capitula,* i.e., *Emendatio Vitae* (ff. 128^v – 132)
10.   *Super Threnos* (ff. 138 – 141)
11.   *Super Orationem Dominicam* (f. 143)
12.   *Super Symbolum Apostolorum* (ff. 143^v – 148)
13.   *Super Lectiones Job In Officio Mortuorum* (ff. 148 – 166)
14.   *Super Magnificat* (f. 167)

It is a paper folio volume written in apparently one hand in the years 1409 (?) to 1411, measuring 12 x 9 1/4 inches with pages 11 1/2 x 8 1/2 inches, containing iv and 170 leaves, each of the latter holding double columns of from 59 to 72 lines of clear, compact script. The book is arranged in fourteen quaternions, beginning with folio 1. Gatherings: i^{14}, $ii-x^{12}$, xi^{10}, xii^9 (originally ^{12}), xiii^{24}, xiv^3. Two paper leaves are bound onto f. 168 to form ff. 169–70 of the present volume. Leaves i–ii are paper, leaves iii–iv parchment; these are marked "i, ii, iii, iv" in pencil. On iii^r in the upper center there is an entry, *"Liber librarii Wigoriensis unde desumptus Mar. 22, 1590 et illuc restituendus."* The catalogue notes that this was written by William Thornhill, prebendary of Worcester, 1584–1626. On folio 1 in the upper right we find *"die martis post nat/ beate marie virginis domini . . ."*; the rest is obscure or cut off. On folio 11^v, *"Anno 30."* On folio 49 in the original hand, *"Anno domini MO CCCC II die mercuri[i] hora 3a post meridiem 13 die Mai."* On folio 87 rubric *"Anno 2o f. iiij."* Allen lists all of the marginalia and annotations of interest; it seems that the manuscript may have had wider margins when she inspected it because some of the entries she notes are no longer visible. There are at least three watermarks resembling a cat; two are very like Briquet's No. 3552 (*Les Filigranes*, Geneva, 1907) but they also have marked differences. All are in the general class 3550–3552 dated early Fifteenth Century, one in 1380. The rubricator and the corrector have worked erratically. Some capitals are illuminated in blue; there are occasional rubrics. The marginal notations, designs, comments, dating, and insertions are interesting for the insights they provide into the working of the scribe. The names "ihu" and "maria" occur at the top and bottom of the pages respectively, the former all the way through, the latter in the opening pages. The paper is in good condition, only slightly faded, but worm holes cause progressively more difficulty from folio 133 on. The volume is bound in brown leather on cardboard with scroll work on the front and back covers; there are five ridges on the spine. Allen's description is the most complete on record; no one else has taken scholarly notice of this manuscript.

B.   **Corpus Christi College MS. 193 (O)** contains twelve Latin works by Rolle and two, the *Speculum Peccatoris* and the *De Tribulacione*, which are often falsely attributed to him. The works include:

1.   *Latin Psalter* (ff. 2ʳ – 110 – 11 [sic])
2.   *Super Lectiones Job In Officio Mortuorum* (ff. 110 – 11 – 135ʳ)
3.   *Super Threnos* (ff. 135ʳ – 142ᵛ)
4.   *Super Cantica Canticorum* (ff. 142ᵛ – 156ʳ)
5.   *Tractatus Super Psalmum Vicesimum* (ff. 156ʳ – 160ʳ)
6.   *Super Orationem Dominicam* (ff. 160ʳ – 161ʳ)
7.   *Super Symbolum Apostolorum* (ff. 161ʳ – 165ʳ)
8.   *Emendatio Vitae* (ff. 165ʳ – 171ʳ)
9.   *Liber De Amore Dei Contra Amatores Mundi* (ff. 171ᵛ – 180ᵛ)
10   *Incendium Amoris* (ff. 180ᵛ – 206ʳ)
11.   *Melum Contemplativorum* (ff. 206ᵛ – 51ᵛ)
12.   *Judica Me Deus* (ff. 251ᵛ – 258ᵛ)
13.   *Speculum Peccatoris* (258ᵛ – 261ʳ)
14.   *De Tribulacione* (ff. 261ʳ – 266ʳ) (f. 266 blank)

It is a vellum book of the late Fourteenth Century, containing i and 267 leaves (but the foliator begins on i with "f. 1"), measuring 10 3/8 x 7 1/2 inches with 41 lines of clear set hand per page up to folio 111ʳ at which point there is a change of hand and 47 lines per page to the end. The second hand is smaller but of the same general variety. The book is arranged in 28 quaternions, beginning with folio 2. Gatherings: i – xiv⁸, xv – xxvi¹², xxvii¹⁰, (originally ¹²), xxviii², (originally ⁴). On f. 267ʳ appears: "*Exp. symboli et Orat Dn. paulo ' arb' lib. de Emend. pcce.*" The verso is blank. On f. 268 there is some inconsequential jotting on the recto; on verso a contemporary librarian's collation. On the inside front cover on parchment pasted to the cover back: "*libri fratris johannis Hanton monachi Ebor–.*" Then there is a half – leaf which is a conjugate of this pasted leaf. Then a whole leaf pasted under the former pasted whole leaf; this is marked "1" in pencil. On the upper center is "E. 2.7" and in the upper right corner, "*v. Catenam Al Lipemanni in Psalm ubi habetur Rich. Pampolitanus.*" This last word suggests a connection of this MS with the printed editions of 1535 or 1536. On the verso of this sheet in middle left is "In Viii ✍ ." The manuscript is colorful and has elaborate illumination. Initial letters of each new work are done in a floral design extending over considerable portions of the adjoining margin in reds, blues, white, and gold. The beginning of each new chapter or section of a given work had a blue letter with a red leaf design extending up and down the margin. Scriptural quotations in capitals underlined usually in red. The MS has been worked over by a corrector and the scribe himself. There are occasional corrections in a later hand, including incorrect incipits, e.g., ff. 180^v, 187, 188^v. The book itself is in good condition, but the cover, of hide – covered boards, has deteriorated. There is evidence of some repair work on the covering. There are the remains of two clasps and evidence on the back cover that a plate or boss was attached. The spine has six ridges with "Ms. CCC 193" below the sixth. On the top of folio 2 appears: "*Opera Richardi Hampole Heremite qui vivit tempore Ed. 3 regis No 1660.*" At the bottom below the text of the Psalter is: "*Arma Robert de Lacy qui fundavit prioratum de Pontefracto*" and then what appears to be the arms.

C.   **Bodley Latin MS. Th. d. 15 (T)** contains a collection of miscellaneous Latin and English works either transcribed by Robert Parkyn, curate of Adwick – le – Street near Doncaster, or written by him. In addition to three works by Rolle, *Super Lectiones Job in Officio Mortuorum* (ff. 1 – 86^v), *Super Mulierum Fortem* (ff. 86^v – 89^r), and the *Tractatus Super Psalmum Vicesimum* (ff. 89^v – 105^v), it contains the following:

1.   "*Genealogia regum Israel a morte Salamonis usque ad transmigrationem Babilonis.*" (ff. 106 – 108^r)

2.   Summary of Pauline epistles. (ff. 108 – 114)

3.   Prayers by St. Thomas More. "Help me dere father" printed by A. G. Dickens from this MS in *Church Quarterly Review*, 247 (1937), 231 – 6. "O holy trinite" printed in *Works* (1557 edition), pp. 1417 seq. [Note: The first page of an unpublished Bodleian catalogue records that the first of these prayers is by St. John Fisher and cites Dickens, *Tudor Treatises*, Yorks. Arch. Soc., 125 (1959).]

4.   A poem. Inc.: "o holly gode of dreydfull maieste"; exp.: "and bring my sowlle to highe salvation." (ff. 119 – 120^r)

5.   "*Sermo ex commentario beati Hieronimi presbiteri*" partly based on Jerome's *Comment. in Matth.* (*PL*, XXVI, 138 – 9). Inc.: "*Grandis fiducia, Petrus piscator erat*"; exp.: "*et in choris sanctorum gratulemur in sec. sec. Amen.*" (ff. 120^v – 121^r)

6.   Latin catalogue of kings of England drawn from Geoffrey of Monmouth and continued by Parkyn. (ff. 121^v – 124)

7.   "Here after followith certen Englishe verses . . . concernyng the Kyngs of Englande sithen the Conquest . . . lattly written by Robert Parkyn . . . *anno domini* 1551 . . . . (ff. 125 – 131)

8.   "*Dietarium salutis*," versified rules of health by John Lydgate (Cf. Brown and Robbins, *Index*). (ff. 132 – 133^r)

9.   Prose account in English of the events of 1532 – 35, printed by A. G. Dickens, *English Historical Review,* LXII (1947), 64 – 83. (ff. 133^v – 141^v)

10.   St. Cyprian's *Epistula ad Fortunatum*, copies from the Erasmus edition. (ff. 142^r – 157^v)

It is a volume of iii and 159 leaves of parchment (i – iii and ff. 1 – 92) and paper (ff. 93 – 159) written by Robert Parkyn at various times before 1565, – measuring 240 x 190 (170 – 180 x 135, ff. 1 – 114^v) mm., containing between 18 – 33 lines in single column.   The book is arranged in 19 quaternions, beginning with folio 1.   Gatherings: i^{12} (^{9} cancelled), ii^6, iii^8 (^{1} cancelled), ivix^8, x – xi^{10}, xviii^8 and ^{1}, xix^6.   Folios 158 – 9 are parchment flyleaves bound in after quaternion 19.   The paper is watermarked with a hand fleur – de – lys and star with initials F. P. (Cf. Briquet, Nos. 11371 – 5). The manuscript is decorated only with plain red initials.   The binding is of brown leather on oak boards with two clasps of which the hasps are now missing.   On folio iii, in Parkyn's own hand (except for the name "Byard" written over an erasure, presumably of "Parkyn") appears: "*Iste liber pertinet ad dominum Robert Byard.*"   The volume belonged to Sir Brian Cooke of Wheatley (Cf. A. G. Dickens' article (58, n. 1); it was purchased in 1931 at

the sale of the library of G. E. Cooke in Yarborough. Scholarly notice was
taken of the manuscript by A. G. Dickens, *EHR*, LXII (1947), 58 – 64.

Other:

A.   **Cambridge, Corpus Christi College MS. 365 (C)** contains the
following Latin works by Rolle:

    1.   *Latin Psalter* with O. T. Canticles (ff. 1^r – 113^v)

    2.   *Super Lectiones Job in Officio Mortuorum* (ff. 114^r – 143^v)

    3.   No title. Inc.: "*Latria est honor soli deo debitus*"; exp.: "*et
sectarie cruci representante crucifixum* . . . " (breaks off abruptly). (ff.
143^v – 144^v)

    4.   *Tractatus Super Psalmum Vicesimum* (ff. 145^r – 152^v)

    5.   *Liber de Amore Dei Contra Amatores Mundi* (ff. 152^v – 168^v)

It is a parchment quarto volume of the Fifteenth Century, measuring 9
1/4 x 6 5/8 inches and containing iii and 168 leaves with an average of 39
lines in single column per page. The three parchment flyleaves at the
beginning are not numbered; at the end there are three paper flyleaves, two
recent, the other later than the manuscript but earlier than the other two.
The foliation is correct, the foliator numbering f. 13 and every twelfth folio
following, i.e., the first leaf of every gathering. It is written in a small but
clear script with initial capitals often illuminated; *Psalmum Vicesimum* begins
with a gold illuminated letter. *Contra Amatores Mundi* has two such capitals.
The normal is a blue capital with red scroll or pen work extending up and
down the margin; in the *Psalter* scriptural quotations begin with a red or blue
capital and are underlined in red. Many corrections and notations appear in
the margins, particularly in the *Job*. "*Ex dono Willelmi warren quondam
maioris Douorrie*" appears on iii^v, and on iv: "*Iste liber* . . . (erasure)." The
volume has been rebound in gray and green, December, 1947.

B.   **Library of Lincoln Cathedral MS. 209 (or C. 5. 2) (L)** contains four
Latin works by Richard Rolle and the *Officium* prepared for the nuns of
Hampole priory. The contents are as follows:

1. *Officium de Sancto Ricardo Heremita* (ff. 2 – 15^r)
2. *Liber de Amore Dei Contra Amatores Mundi* (ff. 15^r – 40^r)
3. *Super Lectiones Job in Officio Mortuorum* (ff. 40^v – 94^r)
4. *Tractatus Super Psalmum Vicesimum* (ff. 94^v – 104^v)
5. *Melos Amoris* (ff. 105 – 214^v)

Folio 1 is blank; scribblings on f. 2. On f. 215 there is a "rough list of the ten plagues"; f. 215^v – 216^v contains scribblings; f. 217 has a list of contents and some verses; f. 217^v is blank. This is a parchment volume of the late Fourteenth Century, measuring 8 3/4 x 5 3/4 inches and containing 217 leaves with a modern paper flyleaf at beginning and end. The leaves are numbered correctly throughout; folio 1 (which was originally the pastedown) and folio 2 are flyleaves although they are numbered with the text. The first 104 folios were transcribed in single column of 28 – 9 lines by John Wodeburgh, the remaining section, comprising the *Melos Amoris*, in double column in a different hand. Gatherings: i^2, ii – iii^9, iv^{10}, v^8, vi^{10}, vii^8, viii^{10}, ix – xii^8, xiii^6, xiv^9, xv^{10}, xvi – xxi^{12}, xxii – xxiii^{11}. The text is rubricated with red capitals on purple pen work or blue capitals on red. The hands are both small and clear, the second more angular than the first. The marginal decoration is simple, generally limited to pendants in the bottom line. There are very few marginalia. The manuscript is in good condition except in the second gathering where chemical stains have almost completely obscured the text.[27] On folio 104^v there appears a short verse within a bracket which begins: "*Hunc Wodeburgh scripsit . . .*"; the bracket is followed by the name "I. Wodeburgh."

C.   **Uppsala Universität Bibliotek MS. 621 (U).** I have not been able to examine directly so the following description is approximate and is based upon Xerox and microfilm copies and upon brief notes in Allen (53, 527 – 9).

Uppsala C. 621 was probably written in Sweden; it was once in the possession of Wadstena, the motherhouse of the Brigittine Order. It is the product of one scribe who apparently also did Uppsala C. 17. MS. C. 621 is a

---

[27] According to Wooley (10) this is the work of G. G. Perry.

volume measuring approximately 8 5/8 x 5 3/4 inches, containing 117 leaves
of text written in single column of from 37 to 39 lines. The hand is quite
compressed and abbreviated, and it becomes progressively more careless
after about forty folios. The film shows that the text has been rubricated and
corrected to some extent. There are almost no marginalia beyond an
occasional "Nota" and the corrections to be inserted. The manuscript
appears to be in good condition.

The contents of the manuscript having to do with Rolle are the following:

    1.   *Tractatus Ricardi Heremite Valde Utilis De Regula Vivendi, i.e.,*
the Emendatio Vitae. (ff. 36^r – 50^r)

    2.   *Tractatus Super Psalmum Vicesimum.* (ff. 55^r – 63^v)

    3.   *Incendium Amoris.* (ff. 63^v – 67^v)

    4.   *Defensorium contra Oblectratorens* [for *oblectratores*] *eiusdam*
Ricardi quod composuit Thomas Basseth sancte memorie. (ff. 67^v – 72^v)

    5.   *Officium de Sancto Ricardo Heremite.* (*lectiones* 1 – 6 abridged)
(ff. 103 – 105)

The Printed Edition:

    The edition printed at Cologne in 1536 (**K**) by Johann Faber of
Heilbronn:

Recto:

D. Richardi Pampolitani Anglosaxonis Eremitae, viri in divinis scripturis ac
veteri illa solidaque Theologia eruditissimi, in Psalterium Davidicum, atque alia
quaedam sacre scripturae monumenta (quae versa indicabit pagella)
compendiosa iuxtaque pia Enarratio. [Followed by the mark of a serpent
entwined around the shaft of an arrow.] *Coloniae, ex officina Melchioris*
Novesiani, Mense Martio, Anno M. D. XXXVI. Cum gratia & privilegio
Caesareo ad Sexennium.

Verso:

[In script]   *Catalogus eorum Quae in Hoc volumine onmia eiusdem authoris lucubraciones continentur.*

[In print]   *In Psalterium Davidicum atque adeo psalmos omnes ennaratio.*
               In Psalmum XX. Domine in virtute tua laetabitur rex, &c.
               tractatus quidam peculiaris
               In aliquot capita Iob
               In Threnos Ieremiae
               In orationem dominicam
               In Symbolum Apostolicam
               In Symbolum Athanasii
               De emendatione peccatoris opusculum
               De incendio amoris
               De amore summo eodemque singulari

Folio ii^r:

Vigilantissimis consulibus ac universo senatorum ordini, Imperialis civitatis Vuympinensis, Joannes Fabri, ab Haylbruñ + Dominicanus.

A letter of dedication follows (to f. ii^v); then an index of topics (ii^v – iv^v):

Ff. I – LXXXIII^v	*Latin Psalter*

Ff. LXXXIII^v – LXXXVIII^v *"Eiusdem D. Richardi in Aliquot Sanctorum Veteris Testamenti mire pia cantica"* (exegesis with head captions: *"Canticor. Biblicos Explanatio"*)

Ff. LXXXIX^r – CXXII	*Super Lectiones Job in Officio Mortuorum*
Ff. CXXIII – CXXIX^v	*In Threnos*
Ff. CXXX – CXXXIV^v	*In Psalmum XX*
Ff. CXXXV – CXLII^r	*De Emend. Peccatoris*
Ff. CXLII – CXLIII^v	*Encomium [Nominis Jesu]*
Ff. CXLIII^v – CXLIIII^r	*De Incendio Amoris*
Ff. CXLIIII^v – CXLV^v	*In hec verba Salomonist.: Adolescentulae, etc.*
Ff. CXLV^v – CXLVI^v	*Orationis Domini*
Ff. CXLVI^v – CL^v	*Symboli Apostolici*
Ff. CLI^r – CLIII^r	*Symboli Athanasii*

There are four (numbered: blank, ii, iii, blank) and 153 folios, each with recto and verso.   The collation runs: Ai – Aii – Aiii to Zi – Zii – Ziii, ai – aii – aiii to ei – eii.   The text ends of an unmarked page of apparently original paper taped in after eii.   The foliation is consecutive except in the following places:

1.   XXXIX – – LIIII – – XLI – – XLIII – – XLIIII – – XLV . . .
2.   XLVIII – – LXXIX – – L – – LI . . .
3.   LVIII – – LX – – LX – – LXI . . .
4.   LXXXIIII – – LXXX – – LXXXVI – – LXXXVIII – – LXXXVIII – – L
XXXIX . . .
5.   CVIII – – CIX – – CVIII – – CX – – CXII . . .
6.   CXLIX – – CXL – – CLI . . .

Foliation ends at folio CLIII, having begun at folio II. On the flyleaf before the title pate is the watermark "MICHALLET." The pages of the text bear the watermark resembling Briquet No. 5031. The binding has ribbed brown leather spines and conventional leather strip with triangular leather corners over board. The remainder is of paper – covered board; it does not seem to be the original binding.

The text of the *Tractatus* is of necessity eclectic in nature; a thorough analysis of all seven witnesses to the text according to the procedure formulated in Vinton A. Dearing, *A Manual of Textual Analysis*, in an attempt to establish a stemma proved only that all the manuscripts were terminal in their lines of descent from the archetype. MSS. Bodley 861 and Corpus Christi College, Oxford 193 do exhibit a sufficient number of similarities and differences from the others to rank them together against the other five, as even a cursory glance through the notes will prove, but there is not enough evidence to establish their stemmatic relationship beyond this point.

The selection of one variant over another is intended to reflect as faithfully as possible Rolle's original text, but, once the area of decision passes beyond meaning and syntax to questions of style, the accuracy of the edition is only as good as the editor's judgment. In the area of style alone the editor has allowed his judgment to be conditioned by the admittedly slight authority of the two aforementioned manuscripts because, first, Bodley 861, which was apparently assembled over a period of years by a scholarly scribe, is the closest thing we have to a "complete works" of Rolle and therefore a bit more than normal scribal attention to detail may have been present; and, second, the style in these two manuscripts in the places where style is the only difficulty seems to be more consistent with the whole that it is in any of the others.

In the process of edition no emendation was required, and the single addition to the text, the completion of a verse from Psalm XX, is contained within angled brackets. All biblical quotations are referred to according to the Vulgate text; italics in the text is reserved for verbatim quotations, and boldface type for the author's citations of words or phrases from Psalm XX. Paraphrases of sources are indicated in the notes by "Cf." All variants, except those of an orthographic nature mentioned below, appear in the notes.

The orthography of the text has been regularized to conform to normal fourteenth–century practice in the case of e for ae and oe and of assimilation in compound words. Because of conflicting manuscript evidence, superfluous h is always retained (e.g., *anhelare, perhennis*), and l always appears for ll (e.g., tolerare) when there is a variable situation. The letter p is always inserted (e.g., *dampnatis*). The following have been regularized for clarity and ease of reading: ti for ci, consonantal v and vocalic u, and qu used for c. Of these three only the last is recorded. Initial I has been regularized to J in proper names. Punctuation, capitalization, and paragraphing are the editor's responsibility.

THE TEXT

Incipit Tractatus super Psalmum vicesimum

     Cum Christus, qui est veritas, dicat: *Sine me nichil potestis facere*, constat sine dubio, quia quicquid boni aut cogitamus, aut volumus, aut
5 loquimur, aut operamur, illud nimirum a Deo habemus. Laudamus ergo et predicamus ineffabilem divine maiestatis clementiam et misericordie magnitudinem; qua non solum peccatores et eterne morti addictos redimere voluit, verum etiam et nos in insula maris magni genitos et nutritos, a faucibus maledicti draconis liberatos, sapientie creatricis dulcedine benignus illustravit.
10 Huius amore tacti et circumligati quasi vinculis insolubilibus, aliena non diripimus, sed conditoris nostri gratiam secure expectamus, dicentes cum Psalmista: *Audiam quid loquatur in me Dominus Deus.* Non utique in nostris viribus presumimus confidere, sed in Deo precipue credimus, cui scimus etiam nosmetipsos nos debere. Illi, inquam, totum tribuimus, a quo nimirum totum
15 habemus; quicquid scimus, quicquid possumus, quicquid sumus ad laudem conditoris nostri totum studeamus redigere, qui pro nobis non solum sua, sed etiam seipsum dignabatur offerre; ut dum toto corde, tota virtute, toto posse nostro, dilectionem Dei desiderare non desinimus, bonis moribus insigniti, et nostrarum affectionum dominatores effecti, secundum Prophete sententiam in
20 Domino gaudeamus: **Domine in virtute tua letabitur rex.**

     Cum omnes psalmi dulces sint et delectabiles, iste psalmus de gloria regis precipue loquitur, consequenter insinuans quod nullus in Domino letabitur sine regimine, nec aliquis recte regitur nisi Deo rectore. Describit ergo Propheta sanctorum gaudium et tormentum impiorum. Delectabuntur namque
25 omnes iusti et sancti in explanatione huius psalmi. Mali vero valde deterreri poterunt, qui se non bene sed male egisse meminerunt.

Rex itaque dicitur vel quia regit vel quia regnat; immo plenius dicatur et
quia regit et quia regnat. Sed rex, de quo sanctus propheta loqui conatur, quid
est quod regit, et super quo regnat, quia tam audacter asserit: **in virtute Domini
letabitur?** Quoniam in virtute Dei nec rex, nec servus letari poterit, nisi rex
5   recte regendo, servus bene obediendo inventus fuerit. Preterea si tantummodo
reges in Deo letari merentur, ubi putas servi et humiles, despecti et pauperes
gloriabuntur? Quippe sine Deo letari non dicatur letitia, sed potius abhominatio
prophana.

Idem igitur Propheta ait: *Parasti in dulcedine tua pauperi, Deus.* Iam
10 liquet non solum regi, sed etiam Deus in dulcore suo locum parat pauperi, quem
nimirum in hoc seculo maxime videt humiliari; ergo conclusio sequitur quod
verus pauper non pauper, sed rex recte vocetur. Aperto igitur intellectu verbi,
multi qui se reges et rectores putant falli probantur dum nomen regis tenere
cupiunt et opus regiminis negligere non tremescunt. Decidunt hinc itaque a
15 regnis suis inopes, qui se et alios nequiter regebant subiectos. Ergo, O Domine,
in virtute tua non quilibet letabitur, sed rex et non quilibet rex.

Quis est igitur ille rex qui letabitur? Aperiamus verbi intentionem et
videbimus, quia congruentius iustum appellabimus regem. O dignatio miranda,
servum Christi regem fieri! Illi enim servire regnare est. O predicanda pietas,
20 despectum in terris cernemus regem regnantem in Deo, gaudentem in celo cum
angelis! Quis umquam ita remunerat servum suum, ita exaltat militem suum,
quem in sua curia regem constituit in eternum? Hic est verus et eternus rex qui
sub se tot et tantos habet reges, sue voluntati penitus conformes. Et ne putet
quis quod tam magni forsitan pauci sint, ait: *Dinumerabo eos et super harenam
25 multiplicabuntur. Vere gloriosa dicta sunt de te, civitas Dei.* Igitur, O bone
Domine, *memor esto Raab et Babilonis scientibus te,* dum inveniri potes. Hinc
pateat liquidum cordibus nostris, quia coram Deo miser mundi non despicitur,
nec honoratus reputatur. Non nocet anime hic deprimi, nec prodest corpori in
terrenis exaltari. Omnes divitie, onmes delitie presentis seculi pro nichilo
30 computantur *ante tribunal Christi. Non enim est acceptor personarum Deus,*
quemadmodum perversitas humana, immo et dementia hominum, que potentes
mundi, non quia homines *ad imaginem et similitudinem Dei* creatos, sed quia

divites, honorat. Hinc probatur miser nec Deo nec hominibus, sed stercoribus reverentiam exhibere, cum ab apostolo divitie stercora vocentur. Iste est *qui adorat sculptilia, et qui gloriatur in simulachris*, et ideo confundetur; quandoquidem et pauperem quamvis sanctum non honorat, sed potius despicit,

5 sub pedibus ponit, et aliam causam non invenit, nisi quia per paupertatem vadit. Sed attende quam infelix et maledictus est. In divite honorat stercus, in paupere contempnit Christum. Nonne legit et audivit: *Quod uni de minimis meis fecistis, michi fecistis?* Pauperem tota die non timet offendere, diviti in omnibus semper cupit placere. Et ecce quid agit dum Christum sibi iratum

10 habere non metuit: *demonis gentium* se coniungit. Caveat ergo sibi unusquisque, quia nisi quis charitate vestitus fuerit in nuditate pudendorum confusus, coram cunctis oculis a nuptiis agni et uxoris eius expulsus erit. Sed ille nimirum maxime confundetur qui de gloria ad penam, de divitiis ad paupertatem transportatur.

15 Proinde timeant perversi pauperes, sed amplius terreantur superbi divites, quia simul in unum dives et pauper, iusto iudici reddent rationes. Minus confunditur pauper qui perit, quia nusquam honoratus fuit, quam dives qui olim in delitiis lasciviens extitit et in divitiis superbivit, vel qui se mundanis honoribus inaniter exaltavit.

20 Beatus ergo rex qui in virtute Dei letabitur, quoniam quidem ab omni confusione culpe et pene perhenniter protegetur. Sed unde rex et ubi regnat, cum Christus dicat non solum pro se, sed etiam pro membris suis: *Regnum meum non est de hoc mundo*? Sane igitur advertendum est, quod illi regi de quo Propheta loquitur, non tantum mundus sed et pariter caro subiungatur. Immo et

25 diabolum firma fide, sincera charitate, viriliter pugnando obruit. Quod Propheta videns, non indigne regem appellavit: O felix rex et plane felix, qui non unum tantum, sed quatuor regna devicit, regnum mundi per paupertatem voluntariam, regnum carnis per temperativam prudentiam, regnum diaboli per humilem patientiam, regnum celi per charitatem perfectam. Ergo *regnum* eius

30 *non est de hoc mundo*, quia gaudium non querit nisi de celo. Cupidus, avarus, superbus, luxuriosus, non vicerunt regna nec obtinuerunt castra, sed ab omnibus devicti sunt et ideo iuste sine regno *in lacum miserie et in lutum fecis* dolentes

cadunt. Ipse autem qui in se vitia consumpsit, *ora leonis rugientis querentis*
quem devoret oppilavit, mundum despexit, carnem spiritui mancipavit; talis
utique rex recte dicitur, cuius potentie ubique obeditur, quia non timet
impugnantem, in Deo iugiter confidens asportare victoriam, clamans cum
5   Psalmista: *Si consistant adversum me castra, non timebit cor meum. Si exurgat*
adversum me prelium, in hoc ego sperabo.

Canamus ergo hilares in laudem Dei, et militis sui iam regis effecti,
dicendo cum Propheta: **Domine in virtute tua letabitur rex.** Hic est rex qui
seipsum recte regit, qui corpus et animam ad servitium Christi constanter
10   dirigit, qui omnes cordis affectiones, omnes mentis evagationes, cuncta animi
desideria tali regimine gubernat, ut de tota interioris et exterioris hominis
habitudine quod non sit ad laudem conditoris dispositum, nichil remaneat. Isti
regi congruit quod alibi dicitur: *Rex sapiens populi stabilimentum est.* Sane rex
populum suum stabilivit qui se totum ad amandum Deum tribuit. Populum
15   istius regis non homines terre, sed cogitationes anime vocamus, que tunc recte
reguntur quando omnes ad gloriam Dei mancipantur. Itaque rex in amore Dei
se totum regens, et super universorum vitiorum maculas potenter regnans,
merito in virtute divina letari perhibetur qui inimicos Christi ut fortis miles
expugnare conabatur. A Deo nimirum et ipse rectus est, et sine ipso vincere
20   non potest. Ergo et bene dicitur, quia in virtute Domini letabitur, non in sua.
Nam fidelis servus gloriam querit Domini, ut etiam in Domino suo et ipse valeat
gloriari.

Quippe qui gloriatur in Domino glorietur, a quo quicquid habet accipit et
sine quo nec quidem subsistit: **Et super salutare tuum exultabit vehementer.**
25   Quando quis plene habet quod bene diligit, proculdubio tunc vehementer
exultabit. Quia enim *charitas non querit que sua sunt*, sed Jesum Christum. In
Jesum salutari Dei electa anima non solum in futuro, sed etiam in presenti
iubilat dum Deum vere et perfecte amat. O singulare donum dilectionis, que
sola eterni regis dulcorem rapere in trepido ascensu transducitur et tante
30   maiestatis suavitate oblectari merentur! Nullus namque gaudet in hoc quod non
amat, et hec est ratio, quia peccatores in Christo numquam letari poterunt quem
nimirum diligere nequaquam voluerunt. Gaudium vero ex amore dilecti

nascitur, et tanto iocundius quis letabitur quanto ferventius Christum amare conatur. Qui pre aliis Deum diligit, etiam in Christo magis letabundus erit. Qui multum amat multum gaudet, et qui minimum amat minimum gaudet. Et qui Christum amare negligit, in illo penitus gaudere nescit, ut secundum

5 quantitatem vere dilectionis unicuique electo retribuatur magnitudo beatitudinis. Mali denique quemadmodum nec volunt esse participes Domini amantium, ita nec erunt consortes in Deo gloriantium. Gloria vero quam perfecte et plene habebimus in patria causatur ex charitate in qua vivebamus in via. Hic namque oportet nos amorem incipere, ut in celo ubi non est terminus amoris valeat

10 permanere. Si ergo in futura vita gloriam cupimus, dum in hoc presenti seculo sumus, Christum toto posse nostro diligere studeamus. Igne charitatis Dominus electorum suorum corda succendit et hoc ad petendum illis suggerit quod ad eternam eorum salutem pertinere prescivit. Inflammati vero divini amoris dulcedine, sola celestia gaudia desiderant que, quia in presenti ad plenum

15 perspicere non possunt, nulli dubium quin in futuro ex bonitate Dei clare et perspicue possidebunt.

Unde sequitur: **Desiderium cordis eius tribuisti ei et voluntate labiorum eius non fraudasti eum.** Regi, id est, sancto cordis sui desiderium Deus tribuit, quia illud quod sibi dare volebat, illum desiderare fecit. Sanctus

20 quippe terrena non cupit sed contempnit; vana mundi non querit gaudia, sed celestia sine fine mansura. Humum non diligit, quia Christus illi dulcescit. In carnalium voluptatum blanditiis non posuit desiderium, sed in spiritualibus delitiis perfruendis figebat cor suum. Deus ergo desiderium suum sibi tribuit, immo magis quam desiderare scivit. Dedit sibi angelorum consortium,

25 sanctorum gaudium, vite eterne beatitudinem, perhennis requiei sedem, veri luminis claritatem, audire melos angelicum, videre incircumscriptum lumen eterni amoris, delitiarum canticum canere mellifluum. Quid ultra restat promere? Dedit ei plenam conditoris cognitionem, in tota Trinitate letitiam. Recte, Domine, servus tuus cordis sui stabilivit desiderium quod **voluntate**

30 **labiorum eius non fraudasti eum.** Idem enim voluntas est labiorum quod et cordis est desiderium. Corde desiderat, labiis clamat, sed et a devotione cordis ascendit in auribus Dei vox orationis. Ergo **non fraudasti eum a voluntate**

labiorum eius, sed misericordissime fecisti, habundantissime implesti, affluentissime satiasti.

     Sed ne quis putet merito suo tam magna sibi fieri sed sola gratia Dei, recte subditur: **Quoniam prevenisti eum in benedictionibus dulcedinis;**
5   **posuisti in capite eius coronam de lapide pretioso.** Non prevenit te, O bone Jesu, iustitia, sed tu prevenisti misericordia. Nisi enim Deus electos quos salvare decrevit gratia preveniret, inter filios hominum non inveniretur quem iustificaret. Inspirat ut recte velit in benedictionibus dulcedinis, subsequitur ut voluntatem perficere possit. Primo igitur predestinatum penis quas pro peccatis
10   suis meruit, deterret, ut vel saltem peccare desistat; et dum horrore tormentorum mala cavet agere, incipit quodammodo seipsum corrigere et, in quantum sensualitas permittit, bona desiderare. Cum vero carnalia desideria mortificare studuerit, quidam sapor celestis in animo iam pene purgato dulcescere assuescit, et *gustato, quoniam suavis est Dominus*, in benedictione
15   dulcedinis se preventum sentit. Ita nimirum fit quod preter illa interna solatia nec aliquid amare aut cogitare querat. Inde exteriora vilescunt; transitoria queque ac omnem mundi inanem gloriam nec appetere curat nec respicere, quia illum solum bene et delicate viventem iudicat qui veraciter Christum amat. Unde timorem expellens ad amorem surgere non desinit, et Christum solum
20   desiderans eius voluntatem incessanter perimplere concupiscit. Iam *inebriatur ab ubertate domus Dei*, ut nil mundane conversationis illi libeat; et igne Spiritus Sancti calefactus eternitatisque amore liquescens, totum cor fervor dulcifluus obumbrat. Accensus ergo superne speculationis dulcedine, crebrius in illud verum lumen mentaliter rapitur; et absorptus divini amoris claritudine et a
25   cunctis presentibus translatus, ad summa elevatur.

    Unde de tali exuto a corpore vel in carne existente ad Christum merito canimus: **Quoniam prevenisti eum < in benedictionibus dulcedinis; posuisti in capite eius coronam de lapide pretioso. >** Magna gloria et non minor laus. Superius audivimus eum in virtute Dei letari, iam sciamus eum in letitia
30   coronari; quia qui prius pro Christo fortiter et letanter certare non timuit, modo victor ad patriam transiens, immarcescibilis gaudii coronam accepit. Namque dum cuncta transitoria transvolantes, in solo Christi desiderio anhelare non

desinimus, a Christo gloriam concupitam percipere non dubitamus. Quamobrem a presentium tenebrarum ergastulo transmigrantes, non indigne ad lucem celestium mansionum gloriose perducimur qui, dum in carne viximus, puro cordis oculo sola supernorum gaudia iugiter contemplari conabamur.

5 Meruit igitur miles Christi coronam, non cuiuslibet rei sed lapidis pretiosi, et plane pretiosi, quia non solum celi verum etiam pretium totius seculi. Iste lapis Christus est qui est salus amantium, refugium pugnantium, corona vincentium, gloria regnantium. In capite ergo vincentis de lapide pretioso corona ponitur quando Christus in dulcore Deitatis victori demonstratur. O quam dulce et

10 delicate iste rex, sanctus Dei! Coronari meruit quem Deus Pater Filio suo dilecto eternaliter coronavit. Quid amplius concupisceret qui de manu Domini tam gloriosum ac preclarum diadema percepisset? Denique gloria Dei apparente esuriens satiabitur, sitiens potabitur, infirmus sanabitur, languens consolabitur, vincens coronabitur, coronatus sine fine letabitur. O lapidem pretiosum, in quo

15 omne pretium invenitur, sine quo nec aliquid appreciatur, qui mortuos vivificat, prostratos resuscitat, laboratos reficit, virtutes seminat, vitia eradicat, mellifluo amoris gaudio animas confortat! O lapidem pretiosum, super aurum et omnem mundi dulcedinem desidero illum! Querendus est iste lapis summa mentis delectatione, retinendus continua devotione, amplectendus ardenti dilectione.

20 Non in loculo reponendus est sed in animo; abscondatur in mente ne rapiatur exteriore vanitate.

Qui hunc lapidem vere diligit, vitam a Deo cupit de qua consequenter subiungitur: **Vitam petiit a te, et tribuisti ei longitudinem dierum in seculum, et in seculum seculi.** Hic aperte docemur quod petenda est vita

25 eterna in qua sine fine gloriemur in celesti patria. Sanctus igitur Dei vitam petiit, quia Christum qui via est veritas et vita toto corde concupivit. Iam fremant et tabescant, contremiscant et ululent iniusti reges, superbi milites, perversi divites, omnes quippe tam laici quam clerici mundana cupidine occupati, qui non vitam petunt sed mortem sibi preparant dum in honoribus

30 vanis adquirendis, delitiis pereuntibus degustandis, divitiis supervacue possidendis, tanto affectu et studio insistere non cessant. Morietur etenim in fetoris amaritudine qui in carnalis amoris blanditer vixit delectatione. Nec videbit divinam gloriam qui terreni honoris dilexit sublimitatem. Proinde quam

cito electus Christi seipsum et mundum intime considerat, visibilia cuncta
postponens, immo pro nichilo computans, solam illam perpetuam ac beatam
vitam a Deo petere festinat.   Quia profecto nimis excecatus est qui in tali
thesauro figit animum quem in brevi termino non ignorat perditurum.   Igitur
5   amator Christi, quamquam in hac vita modicum patitur penitentie, celestem
tamen gloriam ante oculos cordis constituens, divini amoris dulcedine ad
tolerantiam vehementer animatur.   Immo quanto plus verus Christi servus
seipsum in hoc mundo adversitati et humilitati letanter exponere non metuit,
tanto amplius et in presenti gratia amoris replebitur et in futuro in gloria
10   sublimior erit.   Nempe Spiritus Sanctus corda suorum ad omnes passiones pro
Christo sustinendas gaudentia reparat dum, carnales concupiscentias extinguens
et effundens, mentes illorum calore eterne lucis suaviter inflammat.   O dulce
lumen, quam delicatum est gaudium quod in tanto dulcore animas amantium
absorbet, ut eis prorsus iam nulla terrenorum mollities libeat!   O Sancte
15   Spiritus, veni et rape me tibi!   Et bene sanctus nuncuparis qui omnes cum
quibus manere dignatus es sanctos facis!   Amor diceris et vere es qui semper
tuos ad amorem accendis. *Deus meus es tu; doce me facere voluntatem tuam.*
Ure igne tuo renes meos et cor meum; ardeat ignis ille in altari tuo.   Veni,
precor te, O dulcis gloria! Veni, dulcedo suavissima! Veni, dilecte mi! Tota
20   consolatio mea, anime mee languenti pro te salubri ac dulcifluo fervore illabere;
igne tuo penetralia cordis mei incende; et intima queque tua luce illustrando,
mellifluo eterni amoris iubilo universa mentis et corporis depasce.   Tu Deus
noster, vitam a te petenti **longitudinem dierum in seculum seculi tribuisti**,
quia hunc te amare, te querere, tuam voluntatem perficere clementer inspirasti.
25   Gaudeat pauper Christum diligens, tantum et talem inhabitatorem habens.

Non terreatur si dives floreat et ille puniatur, et si in mane brevis
potentie florere cernitur, proculdubio in vespere mortis et miserie arescere ac
decidere penitus cogetur; quippe *quasi flos egreditur et conteritur, et fugit velut*
umbra, et numquam in eodem statu permanet. Mundus stultis ostendit florem,
30   sed in fine non percipient fructum.   Immo quod eis in principio apparebat flos
dulcedinis, in fine sentietur *botrus amarissimus.*   Pro vino quod bibebant
carnalium voluptatum, erit *fel draconum vinum eorum, et venenum aspidum*
insanabile tormentorum.   De quibus conqueritur Christus, dicens: *Adversum me*

loquebantur qui sedebant in porta, et in me psallebant qui bibebant vinum.
Clamabunt utique cum dampnatis: *Quare de vulva eduxisti me; qui utinam*
consumptus essem ne oculus me videret. Multo namque tolerabilior esset pena
illi, si in utero materno suffocatus fuisset quam, egresso ex ventre et recepto
5   baptismate, iterum mortalibus et actualibus involutus criminibus hinc discedat.
Non enim equa pena puniuntur divites epulones et parvuli abortivi. Illos
namque ignis infernalis perpetuo cruciabit; parvulos vero sine gratia baptismali
morientes non nisi perhennis obscuritas tenebit. Letetur igitur qui petit vitam,
non temporalem qua omnino carebit, sed eternam in qua sine fine gaudeat.
10   Quia nimirum non est Christiani honoris exaltari in terrenis, sed potius despici,
humiliari, a mundanis irrideri, maledici, et odiri ut verificetur illud Evangelii:
Eritis odio omnibus hominibus propter nomen meum. Sic vero dilector Christi,
vana et fallibilia predia huius seculi relinquens, ad celestes divitias iugiter
suspiret et, adversa presentis vite letanter patiens, illas internas delitias
15   infatigabiliter degustet.

De quo statim annectit Propheta congratulando, dicens: **Magna est**
gloria eius in salutari tuo; gloriam et magnum decorem impones super
eum. Profecto magnam gloriam in Christo salutari Dei percipit qui Christum
tota cordis dilectione cupit. Quia videlicet, dum sancta mens terrenorum
20   cogitationes tumultuantes a se fortiter expellere studet, et virtutum insignia in se
colligere non desinit, in amoris Christi dulcedine magnam utique letitiam sentit.
Neque vero aliquis in divinitate gaudium poterit capere nisi qui cunctis mundi
vanitatibus et divitiis non torpebat abrenuntiare. Ideo enim est gloria eius
magna nimirum, quia multum dilexit. O amor quam laudabilis es, quam
25   amabilis, quam sine pari, etiam omnibus aliis in comparationem tui postpositis,
desiderabilis! In hoc autem ostendis te valentem, potentem, dominantem. Quia
quicquid homo fecerit, quicquid dederit, quicquid passus fuerit, possunt
remunerari in temporalibus bonis obtinendis vel in minoribus penis percipiendis.
Tu solus es qui iuste remunerari non potes nisi in gloria divine visionis. Verum
30   est ergo quod veritas ait: *Qui diligit me, diligetur a Patre meo, et ego diligam*
eum, et manifestabo ei meipsum. O amor quantum vales qui, dum immensa
opera prophetie et miracula a facie Christi fugiendo delitescunt, tu solus in
curiam eterni regis cum Christo duce intrare non formidas, sed et gloriose

susciperis et cum magno honore ad sedem scandere iuberis. Multi Christum videbunt in humanitate, sed soli amatores Christi cernent in Deitatis dulcore. Nemo presumat de Deo quamvis multa fecit, quia solus gaudebit de salute qui Deum amavit. Et quemadmodum nemo sapiens in vase fetenti liquorem
5 optimum ponit, ita nec Christus, qui sapientia Dei est, nisi immunda anima amorem suum fundit. Cum vero purgata anima divini amoris sentire ceperit dulcedinem, nichil omnino scit desiderare preter Christum. Christum diligit, Christum cupit, ex Christo inardescit, in Christum sitit, Christo suspirat. Penetratur amoris iaculo et audacter dicat: *Amore langueo.* Succenditur
10 medullitus igne Spiritus Sancti, ut merito canat Propheta: **Magna est gloria eius in salutari Dei.**

Tunc quippe Christi gloria in fideli anima magna est quando eternis illecta nulla mundi gloria mulceri potest. Cui pre amoris magnitudine omnia temporalia vertuntur in tedium; cui omnis terrena delactatio apparet
15 nocumentum ita scilicet, ut tanta sit gloria eius in Christo, ut nullam utique valeat consolationem invenire in hoc mundo. Cui solitudo non immerito congruit qui nichil terrenum nichilque humanum sapit. Talis nimirum manet in solitudine, quia longe distat ab hominibus celesti conversatione. Nec potest commisceri societatibus secularium qui solummodo delectatur in gaudiis
20 angelorum. Hic a tumultu solus sedens, sed in Christo glorians, ardet et amat, gaudet et iubilat; charitate vulneratus, amore liquefactus, *canticum amoris canit dilecto*, repletus dulcore suavissimo. Iam non dicit orationes suas sed, in sublimitate mentis positus at amore supernorum raptus, mira suavitate supra se capitur et Deo decantare spirituali organo in mirum modum sublevatur. Non
25 intelligas illum sonum emitti per instrumentum corporale, quia, vigor spiritualis carnem superans, illud canere candor causat conscientie bone et purgate.

Huiusmodi anima tanto gaudio undique suffulta non sentit iniurias, gaudet ad opprobria, ridet ad maledicta, quia quam sola conditoris memoria delectat, nulla mundi molestia seu miseria ab amore perturbat. Iustus enim de
30 iure non dicitur qui memoriam Dei a se, dum vigilat, dilabi sinere non veretur. Quemadmodum autem nullus est locus, nullum est tempus, nullum est momentum in quibus beneficia creatoris nostri in nobis sentire non possumus,

ita nullus sit locus, nullum tempus in quibus Deum presentem in memoria non
habeamus. Ita nempe sine Deo nec subsistere valemus, nec esse, nec moveri,
nec vivere; quomodo quando non fuimus, nosmetipsos non potuimus creare.
Dicamus ergo iugiter: *Ipse fecit nos et non ipsi nos.* Et sicut secundum corpus
5   *sine ipso nichil agimus,* ita et ipsum solum de salvatione anime nostre, sola sua
gratia non meritis nostris exigentibus, laudare debemus. Hinc etenim gloria et
magnus decor super nos imponitur cum, cunctis vanitatibus que ad carnem et
mundum pertinet despectis, in Deo solo gloriamur. Nimirum namque pravam
nescit invenire tristitiam qui celestis suavitatis gustat saporem. Cor quidem
10 quod dulcedo Christi reficit amaritudo mundi non punit. Super omnem igitur
presentis vite stultitiam Dei desideravi sapientiam. Quippe non sentiet fetorem
inferni qui dulciter gaudet in amore Christi. Si ergo in presenti tanta est **gloria
eius in salutari,** ut pro glorie habundantia nichil mundane felicitatis potest
appetere, quanta putas erit in futuro ubi Deus **gloriam et magnum decorem
15 imponet super eum?** Beata ergo anima a carcere corporis exuta et ad celeste
regnum perducta, splendore divine glorie perfunditur, et decore eterni luminis
cum impassibilitatis stola gaudens vestitur. Post generalem vero resurrectionem
in corpore et anima glorificata, sicut sol immo incomparabiliter clarius
refulgens, eterna vita perfruetur.

20   Inde profecto est quod subditur: **Quoniam dabis eum in benedictionem
in seculum seculi, letificabis eum in gaudio cum vultu tuo.** Hoc est gaudium
consummatum coram vultu Dei, perhennem inhabitare sedem.   Bene in
benedictionibus in seculum seculi datur qui contemplando vultum Dei tam
gloriose letificari meretur. Hec sola est visio que mestos letificat, infirmos
25 sanat, debiles confortat, que omnibus vere viventibus vitam donat. Hec visio
gaudium est celi, consolatio mundi. In illa visione refectionis sentiunt requiem
qui, dum in via fuerant, durum pro Deo sustinebant laborem. O vultum
admirabilem qui vita est viventium, gloria letantium, lux illuminatorum, requies
exercitatorum! O dulce gaudium videre Dei faciem! O gloriosum aspectum in
30 splendore maiestatis sue intueri regem seculorum! Ibi erit gaudium *quod oculus
non vidit, nec auris audivit, nec in cor hominis ascendit.* Ibi erit amor
ardentissimus, iubilus dulcissimus, dulcor affluentissimus, quando *facie ad
faciem* Deum videbimus. Hec visio Sancte Trinitatis delectatio est plenissima,

dilectio perfectissima, satietas suavissima. O quam felix est qui toto corde ad illam tendit, qui spretis cunctis mundi et carnis concupiscentiis ad illam visionem constanti animo se attingit! O inestimabile gaudium inter angelos Dei hereditatem percipere! Ille ergo dicere potest cum Psalmista: *Funes ceciderunt*

5   *michi in preclaris; etenim hereditas mea preclara est michi.* Nam *cum dederit dilectis suis sompnum, ecce hereditas Domini, filii; merces, fructus ventris. Ibi calix meus inebrians quam preclarus est.* Ubi rex est veritas et vita, lex, charitas, infinita possessio, gloria semper habita et semper appetita. Ibi iugiter nova iocunditas, iocunda felicitas, felix eternitas, eterna securitas, secura

10   delectatio, delicata dilectio, dilecta visio, visio conditoris sempiterna, desiderabilis perfruitio. Hoc est vitam habere beatam istam, sine fine possidere gloriam. Ve qui breviter peccant et illam irrecuperabiliter amittunt! Ve qui potius appetunt peccatorum ponderibus in lacum cum diabolo cadere quam caste et humiliter vivendo Christum in veritate amare! Valde ergo felices sunt qui a

15   sede temporalis miserie ad sedem requiei eterne transmigrant. In illis nimirum eternis sedibus gaudium nostrum erit plenum, quia, Christum in decore suo intuentes, glorie amplius non possumus percipere additamentum.

O Jesu bone, quis michi det ut sentiam te, infunde te in visceribus anime mee! Veni in cor meum et inebria illud dulcore tuo. Reple mentem meam

20   fervore amoris tui ut, omnia mala obliviscens, te solum complectar; certe tunc gaudebo. Amodo ne recedas a me, quia sola tui presentia michi solatium est, sola tui absentia me tristem relinquit. Igitur morare mecum iugiter in tabernaculo meo nam tecum eternaliter letari spero in regno tuo. Quemadmodum quoque a memoria mea dum vigilans fuero, absens non es; sic

25   nec dulcedo amoris tui ab anima mea aliquatenus separetur. Et quomodo hec nullam preter te delectationem affectat assumere, ita continuo laboret studio ut tuam consolationem indesinenter donetur presentire, quatinus, dum in nulla vanitate presentium rerum delectari appetit, presto sit ei *memoriam habundantie suavitatis tue eructanti* dulcedo futurorum, quam cupit. Non mireris igitur, si

30   gaudeat qui divino amori eligitur et supernorum iubilo contemplativus esse inspiratur; sed nec quidem mirabile videtur si verus Christi amator, ad mortem perventus, amplius letificetur. Quoniam non mori putat, sed potius vivere, quandoquidem non ignorat ad Christum, quem solum desideravit, se transire.

Iste nimirum est rex de quo adhuc Propheta loqui non trepidat et tanta gloria dignum esse audacter affirmat. Unde et subdit: **Quoniam rex sperat in Domino; et in misericordia Altissimi non commovebitur.** O potentem regem qui servos suos etiam reges facit et in se tam firmiter fundat confidere quod

5 nulla illos molestiarum instantia permittitur turbare! Unde Apostolus: *Quis separabit nos a charitate Dei? tribulatio? an angustia? an gladius? an fames? an nuditas? Certus enim sum quod neque mors, neque vita, neque alia creatura separabit nos a charitate Dei que est in Christo Jesu.* Recte igitur et vere in Domino et **in misericordia Altissimi** sperare perhibetur qui ab illa re quam spes

10 expectat **non commovebitur.** Multi enim dicunt se sperare in Domino et in veritate non sperant, sed veraciter mentiuntur, quia mala opera, non spem sed desperationem in Domino, manifeste in tremenda discussione ostendent. Et ideo quia tales nec reges sunt neque in Domino sperant, stare non possunt sed commovebuntur et peribunt. Porro satis evidenter describitur regem, id est

15 iustum sperantem in divina misericordia, non commoveri qui in Deo incommutabili et immobili bono desideravit figi, quia qui in Deo non figitur in fallibilibus et transitoriis collocatur. Sed fallacia contra naturam non agunt; ergo omnes ad illos deditos decipiunt. Talem denique oportet cadere qui in cadendis rebus seipsum non timuit fundare. Fragile nimirum et deceptorium

20 fundamentum est concupiscentiis presentium divitiarum: qui illis adheret non dubitet utique moveri. Putredinis namque habet stationem qui in terrenis acquirendis mentis posuit fundamentum. Mundanus ergo miser iuste a suis desideriis commovebitur qui semper vana et insolida, iniuste et supervacue, congregare conabatur. Hiis itaque cadentibus, quam felix est qui commoveri

25 non poterit, qui in eternum in domo Dei perseverabit. Hic est *qui post aurum non abiit, nec in thesauris terrene pecunie speravit*; fundatus erat sine dubio super petram: id est, finem desiderii sui radicavit in Christum; stabilitus in Deo non commovebitur cum hoc mundo. Multa possunt dici super hoc verbo: **non commovebitur,** sed interim sufficiant pauca.

30 Tria ex beneficio creationis quantum ad corpus habemus, scilicet currere vel ambulare, stare et sedere. Si currendo aliquod spectaculum consideramus, manifestum est quod illud plene non perspicimus, quia nimis moti sumus. Stando autem illud bene cernimus, sed quia diu infatigati stare non possumus,

stationem a motu non multum distare non dubitamus. Sedendo vero et
perspicue illud videre poterimus et videndo delectari valemus, quia sedere satis
commune est et diu sine cursu vel statione haberi potest. Si quis habeat a quo
multum se noverit diligi, quia iuxta illud quod multum diligimus multum
5   sedere, non currere vel stare, solebamus. Deus nimirum ex naturali primordio
obiectum est anime; ergo fidelis et devota anima nichil preter Deum pre oculis
suis cupit habere. Ubi est amor, ibi utique est oculus. Nam illud quod
specialiter diligimus, ad videndum et habendum indesinenter anhelamus. Itaque
cum quis Christum amat, iugiter ad Christum intuendum elevari suspirat. Sed
10   dum terrenis quasi currendo distrahitur, vel dum quasi stando minus adhuc
contemplari oblectatur celestia, nequaquam recte est sapiens. Igitur sedens et
quiescens, fit anima prudens. Hinc profecto liquet, quia anima, que amorem
Christi in se et ante oculos suos fideliter et veraciter constituit, iam corpus suum
ad sessionem trahere non desistit. Unde cum nos primum peccata odientes
15   Deum amare incipimus, tunc proculdubio, nisi quasi currendo illum videmus, ac
postea *gustato, quia suavis est Dominus*, statim totum mundum relinquimus; et
ita spiritu Christi super mel dulce ad nos intrante, maiori delectatione illecti,
quasi ad vivendum Deum stamus. Ad ultimum vero eterni amoris dulcore
inflammati, ad canorum quoque iubilum sublevati, quietem mentis et corporis
20   incessanter cupimus ut continue sessioni perpetua visione gaudeamus. Sane hec
est perfectissima vita, sanctissima et angelis similima, sed et celesti suavitate
plenissima quam puto inter mortales quempiam posse comprehendere. Nimirum
perpauci ad hanc pertingunt. In hoc autem ardens et perfectus amator Christi
verissime cognoscitur si per totum diei noctisque spatium sedere delectetur.
25   Divinus namque amor illum compellit quiescere, ut totus homo superne
dulcedinis repleatur iubilatione. Ideo ait Psalmista: *Concupiscit et deficit anima
mea in atria Domini; Cor meum et caro mea exultaverunt in Deum vivum.* Non
mireris igitur si iugiter sedere potuit qui celestium gaudiorum consolamine tam
suaviter inebriatus fuit. Sedendo enim canit et iubilat ac superni amoris
30   suavitate crebro rapitur et, in eternorum contemplatione stabilitus, mirabiliter
iocundatur. Unde de illo merito clamat Propheta: **Quoniam rex sperat in
Domino et in misericordia Altissimi, non commovebitur.** Moveri non potest,
quia in Deo perfecte radicatus est. Inde alibi dicitur: *Ego autem dixi in
habundantia mea,* scilicet charitatis, *non movebor in eternum.* Quia nimirum

unusquisque electus tanto stabilius ponitur quanto in vero amore perfectius
radicatur.

Non miror igitur, si pulsatus temptatione cito cecidit qui in vera charitate
Dei delectatus et suffultus non fuit.   Unde dicitur verissime de hiis qui ficte
5   Christum amant: *Spuria vitulamina non dabunt radices altas, nec stabile
*firmamentum collocabunt. *Et si in ramis in tempore germinaverint, infirmiter
posita, a vento commovebuntur, et a nimietate ventorum eradicabuntur.*   Et ne
putet quis tantam esse bonitatem et misericordiam Dei in iustis et sanctis ut non
exerceatur iustitia eius in malis, ecce descripta gloria beatorum statim ad
10   vindictam reproborum sermonem suum vertit, dicens: **Inveniatur manus tua
omnibus inimicis tuis; dextera tua inveniat omnes qui te oderunt.**   Hec est
prophetia et condelectatio iusti iudicii Dei.   Non enim Propheta iustus postest
velle quod peccatores et luxuriosi vivant diu in iniquitatibus suis.   Sed sciendum
est quod sunt inimici Christi.   Et qui sunt?   Qui illum oderunt; utique qui odiunt
15   inimici sunt.   Et nequaquam aliquis habet inimicum a quo non habet odium.
Inimici ergo Christi sunt falsi Christiani qui Christum, quem in Baptismo
susceperunt, iam in cordibus suis occidere conantur.   Alioquin non diceret
Paulus: *Vivit vero in me Christus.*   Illi non habent Christum vivum in se sed
extinctum et mortuum in peccatis suis, *quia fides sine operibus mortua est* et
20   gravius peccant quam Judei ipsum crucifigentes.   Sed profecto *Christus
resurgens ex mortuis iam non moritur, quod enim vivit vivit Deo.*   Hiis nimirum
mors et miseria appropiat, quatenus dolor eorum et iniquitas super capita sua se
convertat.   Inimicis namque Christi iudicium Dei invenietur, et eterna punitio
inveniet illos, quia in tormentis absque termino morientur, et numquam mori
25   poterunt qui in peccatis suis Deum offendendo semper vivere voluerunt.

Nullus itaque sani capitis de impunitate presumat quoniam mortale
delictum, quod in hac vita non dimittitur, a manu Dei inventum sine fine in
inferno punietur.   Unde et dum mortales miseri, vanis presentis vite curis dediti,
iugiter terrenis lucris inherere cupiunt, gaudia mundi que dilexerant amittentes,
30   ad inferorum incendia que vitare volebant dolentes descendunt, ut quod iam
sequitur in eis impleatur: **Pones eos ut clibanum ignis in tempore vultus tui;
Dominus in ira sua conturbabit eos, et devorabit eos ignis.**   Hec est pena

inimicorum, hec est vindicta odientium Christum. Ve peccatoribus! Ve peccare
volentibus quorum divitie vertuntur in paupertatem, sanitas in morbum, delitie
in fetorem, pulchritudo in deformitatem, dulcedo in amaritudinem, gloria in
ignem, et merito utpote *qui mutaverunt gloriam suam in similitudinem vituli*
5   *comedentis fenum!* **Pones eos ut clibanum ignis in tempore vultus tui.** O
dira sors peccatoris cum ad iudicium venerit; in tota eius substantia intus et
extra flamma ignis infernalis succenditur et, eternis miseriis deputatus, in
carcere tenebroso perhenniter includetur! Et iuste qui ut clibanus igne mundane
concupiscentie, dum presentibus interfuit divitiis, exarserit, abstractus prorsus
10 ab hiis que amaverat ad ea que non timuit, decidens supplicia, in exustione ignis
inextinguibilis semper ardens erit, ut eterne mortis absorptus voragine multo
amplius in cruciatibus suis sibi displiceat quam antea umquam in peccatorum
suorum oblectamentis sibi placere potuerat. Gratulatur enim iniquus cum
malefecerit et cum conceptam libidinis cupidinem se posse explere cognoverit;
15 non modicum venenosi serpentis hasta pervicaci transfoditur ut ad mala
perpetranda que voluerat, oblitis Dei iudiciis, ardenti desiderio deducatur. Sic
vero dum prestigiatoris callidi temptamentis assensum tradere non metuit,
animam propriam in lacum miserie et in lutum fecis sponte demergit. Hoc
nempe malum est, immo pessimum, quod cernimus cum concupiscentias et
20 cogitationes nostras perversas nec timore iudiciorum Dei nec dolore
tormentorum refrenamus sed, dum delectatio coram oculis nostris corporalibus
exponitur, sententia equissimi iudicis a consideratione cordis penitus occultatur.
Sentientes igitur reprobi carnalium delitiarum dulcedinem, longe ab omni
spirituali gaudio repulsi, iam dira morte percussi in terram, titubant; et
25 voluptatibus suis terrenis solummodo inherentes, nichil stultius esse quam
innocenter et iuste vivere putant. Unde et non sine merito: **Dominus in ira sua**
conturbabit eos quem placatum habere numquam desideraverunt. **Et**
devorabit eos ignis, scilicet infernalis, quos prius ignis luxurie et cupiditatis
devoraverat. Tales utique miseri, quia celestibus terrena preponere gaudent,
30 cunctis bonis operibus suis pro nichilo computatis, post mortem desperabunt, ut
testatur Sapiens: *Qui amat*, inquit, *divitias, fructum non capiet ex eis.*

Unde et recte subditur: **Fructum eorum de terra perdes, et semen**
eorum a filiis hominum. Heu miserabilis fructus! Quo amisso, invenitur

luctus; lugebit mundus perdito quod diligit; cruciabitur iniquus invento quod non putavit. Florent mundani dilectores in iuventute dum carnali amori ac terrene cupidini se exhibent; sed quando fructum ferre presumpserint, florem et fructum totum amittent. Flos mundi dulcis cernitur sed, ne dulciter fructificet,

5 cito excidetur. O quam *fallax gratia et vana est pulchritudo* ista! Quid est flos carnalis forme nisi vana veritas, et vera vanitas omne transitorium vere dicatur. Vanum ergo omnis mundi gloria est, vere vana et vane vera, oculos solicitans et animam veneni poculo inebrians. Non recordamur: *quoniam pulvis sumus. Homo sicut fenum dies eius; tamquam flos agri sic efflorebit.* Florem feni

10 respice et huiusmodi hominis florem poteris invenire. Quippe carnalis homo iam propter peccatum suum vanitati similis factus est et *iumentis comparatus insipientibus*, et ideo fructus eius de terra, scilicet vite, perditur et **semen eius a filiis hominum**, videlicet bene viventium, dampnabiliter dissipatur.

Et iuste quidem: **Quoniam declinaverunt in te mala; cogitaverunt**

15 **consilia que non potuerunt stabilire.** In te, ideo per te, quia *non est potestas nisi a Deo.* Nempe et tiranni, perversi divites, pauperum oppressores, iniqui principes, et alii quam plurimi seu predones, quamquam aliena iniuste, unde prosperentur in carnalibus delitiis et adversa mundi evitent, diripiunt; tamen non nisi per Deum, id est per potestatem a Deo traditam, quamvis voluntatem

20 malam a suis concupiscentiis habeant, hec acquirunt. Et si omnino contrarientur voluntati conditoris, ipse ad illorum perniciem bona temporalia eis largitur. Peccatores igitur et delicati in Deo mala declinant, quia nimirum per prosperitatem a Deo datam mundi adversitates tolerare toto corde contradicunt. Videmus enim, quia omnes amatores seculi, sitim, famem, frigus, omnino in

25 quantum possunt declinant; et si temptati fuerint, non stant sed cadunt. Sic profecto patet, quia fugiunt et odiunt bona que accelerant ad celum et diligunt mala et faciunt que ducunt ad infernum. O stultos mercatores et insensatos qui, dum penitentiam cavendo se lucrari iactant, seipsos pauperrimos et miserrimos, non solum omni bono spoliatos verum etiam in malorum profundo

30 deiectos, coram summo iudice demonstrant!

Amatores denique Christi hoc diligunt quod odiunt amatores mundi, nam adversa presentis vite pro Christo etiam gaudent suscipere, sed sine dubio omnia

mala que sunt vitia et anime inquinativa in Christo cupiunt declinare; id est per
amorem et adiutorium Christi peccata constanter fugiunt dum in aliis malis,
scilicet fame, siti, frigore, nuditate, se pro bono suo torqueri cognoscunt; quia
si virtus in infirmitate perficitur, nimirum perfectus in virtute ab omni
5   infirmitate liberatur.   Male igitur mundani miseri declinant malum, quia, dum
se putant malum evadere, mala infernorum non cessant penetrare.   Causa
subiungitur: **Quoniam cogitaverunt consilia que non potuerunt stabilire.**
Superbus namque in superbia sua stabiliri non poterit, quia Lucifer, in celo
superbiens, subito in profundum inferni deiectus fuit.   Nec dives in divitiis suis
10 stabilimentum percipiet sed, ipso dire mortis vulnere percusso, tota gloria
domus eius velut fumus evanescet.   Neque vero carnalis amator voluptatibus
carnis serviens stabili cursu valebit ludere, quia caro deficiet, deformitas
superveniet, mors immisericors rapiet, ut cogatur peccator deinceps gemere,
amplius non exultare.   Sic nimirum: **Cogitant consilia que non potuerunt**
15 **stabilire.**   Quoniam non stabunt consilia impiorum, sed peribunt potius in
iudicio regis seculorum.

Quod notatur in hoc quod sequitur: **Quoniam pones eos dorsum.**   Raro
reminiscitur illud quod post tergum ponitur.   Ideoque Deus inimicos suos
dorsum ponet, quia dampnatos in dolore perpetui ignis, detrusos clementia
20 pietatis sue, sine fine respicere non intendet.   Et quasi post dorsum positi et
penitus obliti, solatium non sentient sed, ac si essent semper ante faciem
vindicantis, dampnati dolebunt.   **In reliquiis tuis preparabis vultum eorum,** id
est corpora eorum cum animabus suis cruciabuntur cum demonibus, impleta in
eis sententia irrevocabili, qua dicitur: *Ite maledicti in ignem eternum qui*
25 *preparatus est diabolo et angelis eius.*   Quot in mundo habuerunt oblectamenta
illicita, tot in inferno tormenta habebunt sempiterna.   Hinc aperte ostenditur
quod inter demones torquebuntur mali homines.

Nimirum et inter choros angelorum gaudebunt consortia sanctorum.
Quorum gloriam et exultationem sicut in principio Propheta posuit, ita et in fine
30 confirmans, dicit: **Exaltare, Domine, in virtute tua; cantabimus et psallemus**
virtutes tuas.   Quasi diceret: Ostende te exaltatum in sanctis tuis quos in virtute
tua supra terrena queque conscendere fecisti.   Quia profecto dum amore

invisibilis glorie divinitus rapimur, magnalia virtutum Dei cantare et psallere medullitus delectamur. Et hoc in presenti per gratiam et in futuro per gloriam, ut ipsum amemus, ipsum laudemus, in ipso gloriemur in secula seculorum. Amen.

SUBSTANTIVE VARIANTS

*MSS B O L T C U K

B: Incipit Tractatus super Psalmum 20^m.

O: Incipit Tractatus super Psalmum 20^m.

L: No title.

T: Hic incipit Tractatus super Psalmum vicesimum editus a devoto Ricardo Roylle quondam heremita de Hanepulle qui migravit ab hoc seculo ad dilectissimum suum Jesum. Anno domini M^o CCC^o xlix^o apud Hanepulle predictus.

C: Glosa Ricardi Hampol super psalmum vicesimum.

U: Incipit tractatus super psalmum XX, scilicet, domine in virtute.

K: D. RICHARDI PAMPOLITANI EREMITAE, IN PSALMUM XX. Domine in virtute tua, &c. peculiaris quædam, atque fusior, quam ENARRATIO.

Page 1

Line

4.   volumus] colimus L

6.   ineffabilem *om* L| divine] //// T

7.   quia T| et *om* LT

8.   et^1 *om* K

9.   creationis L

10.   quia T

13.   presumimus *om* L| confidemus L| in] a LTCUK| precipue] percipere LT| etiam scimus B| etiam *om* L et T

14.   totum^1 *om* L

15.   quicquid^3] et quod U| quicquid sumus *om* T

16.   quia L| pro *om* BO| pro nobis *om* U

17.   etiam *om* L et T| afferre BO

18. insigni T
20. *post* gaudeamus *add* Explicit Prologus T
21. sint dulces LT| sint] fiunt BO fuerint UK sunt C
22. innuans T| letabitur] delectabitur C
23. nec] ne T| nisi] sine BO| ergo] enim C
25. vero valde] autem BO siquidem U| vero *om* L| valde *om* K
26. se] sic L

Page 2

Line

1. quia^2 *om* U| immo . . . regnat *om* L
4. Quoniam] quia U
5. tantummodo] tanto modo T
6. despecti et pauperes *om* BO
10. *post* liquet *add* quod K
11. humiliari] tribulari U
14. Decident L| itaque] utique L
15. regnis . . . nequiter *om* O
17. igitur] ergo T *om* U
18. appelamus U
20. cernimus BO
21. ita *om* L| suum^1 *om* K
22. constituet BO
23. penitus *om* U| quis putet U
24. *post* pauci *add* sancti L| sint] sunt U
26. Domine] Jesu L| scienter BO scientium L| invenire T|
27. liquidum *om* U| miser mundi coram Deo BO
28. corpori *om* U
31. potentem BO
32. creati K

Page 3

Line

1. honorant B| probantur B

3.   *post* simulachris *add* suis U

5.   per *om* B

6.   *post* est *add* qui U| stercora T| pauperem T

7.   de] ex L

8.   *post* michi fecistis *add* mihi fecistis B

10. demonium U| *post* se *add* constituit et U| ergo] igitur BU

13. *post* penam *add* et UK| de vitiis K

16. simul] similiter O| iudice T| rationem U

18. extitit et in divitiis *om* U

19. inaniter *om* BO

20. ergo] igitur LU

23. *post* meum *add* inquit CT| *post* de *add* de O

24. caro pariter BO| *post* pariter *add* et TU| subiugatur K

25. obruit *om* U

26. *post* regem *add* huiusmodi BO

27. *post* regnum *add* videlicet U

28. temperativam] temperantium et BO

29. humilem *mut ad* humilitatem L

30. de] in U

31. *post* superbus *add* et BO| nec] sed U

32. iuste sine regno *om* U| lutum] lacum B

Page 4

Line

1.   rugentis U| *post* rugientis *add* et BO

3.   qui BLUK

5.   propheta T

6.   ego *om* U

7.   Conamus T| ergo] igitur U| milites K| sui . . . dicendo] iam
     regis eterni effecti dicamus K

10. affectiones cordis L

11. et exterioris *om* B

12. nichil] michi C vel L| remanet U

13. cogruit B

15.   terre vocamus sed cogitationes anime qui U

16.   regitur L| *post* omnes *add* homines L| omnes] homines T

17.   maculas vitiorum L

18.   prohibetur BOLT

20.   *post* potest *add* tunc CT| *post* letabitur *add* et BO| in^2 *om* O

21.   etiam] et L *om* K

23.   quicquid habet accipit] quicquam accepit habet T

25.   Quando] Quoniam L| quis] quidem CL| bene] plene L| tunc *om* K

26.   enim *om* B|In *om* C

27.   Jesum] Jesu LTCUK| salutare BOT

29.   rapere] capere U| assensu BO| transducitur] dicitur C

31.   et *om* K| letare L

32.   valuerunt L noluerunt T

Page 5

Line

1.   quis] quisque L| frequentius U

2.   Deum] verum Christum L| etiam] et TK| Christo] eo C ipso LTUK

3.   *post* Qui *add* ergo L| amat . . . minimum^1 *om* O| amat^1] diligit C

4.   gaudere penitus L

5.   dilectionis verae L| tribuatur L

6.   Mali] Quod alii C| Domini] Deum LK

7.   vero quam] enim quamvis L

8.   namque] vero L

10.   hoc *om* BO| seculo *om* LTCU

11.   Dominus] Deus U

15.   prospicere TK

17.   eius *om* C

18.   cordis sui desiderium] desiderium cordis eius L

21.   *post* fine *add* per U| Humanum U| Humum. . . dulcescit *om* L

23.   delitiis *om* BO

26. laritatem O
28. eis L| trinitatem BO
29. *post* recte *add* O U| quod] quia CT
30. est voluntas BOL
31. est *om* B
32. Non ergo K

Page 6

Line

1. eius *om* B| fecisti *mut ad* fovisti U| fecisti . . . satiasti]
sanasti B
2. satiasti] sanasti OK| satiasti *mut ad* sanasti U
4. *post* dulcedinis *add* et U
5. O *om* U| bone] Domine L
6. *post* Jesu *add* Christe L| Deus *om* L
7. decreverit C
8. iustificaretur L
9. igitur] ergo BO sibi K
10. *post* vel *add* sic B| desistit U| horrere T
11. cavent U
12. vero] ergo U
13. quidem T
14. in] et U| benedictionibus L
16. quereat T
17. quoque CL
18. indicat O
19. ad . . . desinit] surgit ad amorem L| *post* amorem *add* Dei
BO| surgit U
20. incessanter *om* L
21. Dei *om* O| Spiritus Sancti igne U| Sancti Spiritus L
22. *post* liquescens *add* se L| *post* cor *add* cor O| cor *om* L
23. obumbrat] inebriat L| ergo] igitur U| illud] idem U
24. verum] verbum K| lumen *om* LTCUK| rapiatur C
27. in . . . pretioso] etc BOLTUK *om* C

29.   audimus U| *post* eum² *add* in virtute . . . eum O

31.   in marcessibilis C| accipit U| Dum namque LTCU | cuncta
       nanque K

Page 7

3.   lucem] laudem U| vixerimus BO

4.   iugiter *om* O| contemplare T

5.   Christi miles L| et plane pretiosi *om* O

6.   celum BOUK| etiam] et K

7.   qui est *om* O| vincentium] viventium KT

8.   ergo] vero CT

9.   Deitatis] Divinitatis KT

10.   *post* rex *add* scilicet O| suo Filio U

11.   eternalem T| conspiceret BO

12.   apparenter B

13.   saturabitur L| *post* consolabitur *add* et L

15.   appreciabitur L

16.   laborantes U laborentes K

18.   mentis *om* L

19.   delectatione] delectionis intencione L| dilectione] delectatione
L

20.   absconditur T| ne] non BOCT

21.   exteriori BCT

22.   consequenter] congrue L

23.   longitudinem . . . seculi *abbr* LU

25.   Dei *om* K

27.   tabescat O| tabescant et U| ululant L

29.   qui *om* K| in *om* BO

31.   tanto] toto U| etenim] enim L

32.   fetore amoris *mut ad* fetoris B| blanditer amoris L|
      blandenter T| delectatio O

33.   quam cito] quanto U

Page 8

Line

1.   cuncta *om* B

2.   vitam perpetuam ac beatam BO

3.   a *om* B| nimis] vitiis C

4.   quem] quod U| *post* ignorat *add* se K

7.   verius T| servus Christi U

8.   seipsum *om* BO| *post* humiliati *add* seipsum BO| non *om* BO

9.   implebitur T

10.   corta O

13.   quam] quoniam L| es LTUK

14.   absorbes UK| terrenorum nulla L| libet BOCTU

15.   et[1] *om* BOUK| rapi T

16.   manere] habitare L| Amor . . . es] Et vere amor es et diceris LTCUK

18.   ille ignes C ignis iste T

19.   *post* Veni[1] *add* precor O

20.   mea] m U| fervore] amore L supernore T

21.   incendi T

22.   melliflua K

23.   *post* noster *add* a te L te BOCK et T

25.   Gaudiat B gaudet U| pauper] semper U

26.   refloreat BO| in *om* LK

27.   potenciem O| ac] et BO

28.   decedere L

29.   stultus L| florem ostendit U

30.   in principio quod eis T

32.   et] erit U

33.   De] Ex U

Page 9

Line

2.   Clamabant BU

4.   *post* quam *add* quod K| egressus K| ex] de L| recepto] accepto BO

5.   iterum] interim U

6.   ponuntur T

7.   vero *om* TK

8.   morientes *om* LTCUK| Letatur T| igitur *om* U

9.   gaudebit U

10.   *post* despici *add* et L

11.   odiri] odio haberi U| Evangelicum C

12.   omni homini LTCUK| vero] ergo U

13.   seculi] mundi U

16.   annectit] amittit O| gratulando BOLU

19.   dum] dicitur B

20.   timultu ñantes C| insigna B

22.   vero] enim BOL

24.   dilexit multum BO| diligit L

25.   pare L| etiam] in T| comparacione LK| positis L

26.   autem] enim L| volentem L

27.   homo *om* U| *post* fuerit *add* quis U| possit U

28.   in . . . remunerari *om* C| vel] et C| in *om* B| mitioribus LU

29.   *post* Tu *add* enim L

30.   ergo] hoc T| ego *om* BO| diligam] diligo U

31.   ei *om* O| qui] que B

33.   sed *om* CL

Page 10

Line

1.   cum] tamen O

2.   *post* cernent *add* eum L ipsum U| Divinitatis KT

4.   amat B

5.   optimum] suum fundit cum vero purgato optimum liquorem U| nec *om* BO| est Dei LTCUK

6.   amorem . . . anima *om* O| suum *om* U| *post* suum *add* non L| divini] Dei K

7. diligit Christum cupit Christum U
8. Christo[1]] ipso C quo U | *post* sitit *add* Christum K | Christo[2]]
   Christum LU | *post* suspirat *add* et L
9. et] ut K *om* L
10. *post* ut *add* de illo BO | *post* canat *add* cum CU
11. *post* salutari *add* et L | salutare T
12. quando] quoniam T
13. electa KU | pre . . . cui *om* U
17. *post* nichilque *add* in L | manet] nec B
18. celestis conversatio U
19. solomodo LT | gaudio K
20. gloriaris O
22. dulcore] amore L
23. supernorum *om* BO | se capitur] rapitur K
25. intelligens L
26. *post* superans *add* est BO | candore U
27. ubique U
28. quam] quem CU
29. miseria seu molestia BO
30. dum vigilat a se L
32. possimus K

Page 11

Line

1. fit CK | presentem Deum BO
2. valeamus TUK
3. non potuimus nosmetipsos U | non[2]] nec T
5. et *om* T
7. carmen C | mundum et carnem T
8. dispectis BO | solo *om* U
10. mundo T *om* U
11. sentit T
13. glorie] gloria T
15. ergo] igitur TU

16. gratiae L
17. impossibilitas L| vero] ergo U
18. clarius *om* BO
19. prefulgens BO| fruetur T perfruatur U
20. Quoniam dabis] Quis dabit B| *post* eum *add* eum O
21. *post* seculum *add* in U
23. quia U| vultu T
24. glorioso C| letificare L
27. pro Deo *om* BO| sustinuerunt L sustinebunt T| vultum]
     multum T| *post* vultum *add* tuum O
28. admirabile OT| es T| luminatorum U
31. videt T| est U| ardentissimus amor U
32. *post* ad faciem *add* ad faciem O
33. videmus LTCUK| sancti B sancto C| delectatio] dilectio L

Page 12

Line

1.   dilectio] delectatio U| dilectio perfectissima *om* O| satietas]
     societas U| suavissumum O
2.   tendit . . . illam *om* U
3.   *post* O *add* quam T| Dei *om* B
4.   Ille . . . Psalmista] Unde U *om* LTCK| ergo] igitur O
6.   suis *om* L
7.   rex *om* T| vita] via U
9.   *post* nova *add* nova O
10. delectatio] delecta O| delicata] delectata K| visio² *om* B|
     post sempiterna *add* et BO
11. fruitio T| vita B
13. appetunt *om* LTCUK| *post* ponderibus *add* volunt U| cum
     diabolo cadere in lacum U| *post* cadere *add* eligunt K
14. ergo] igitur U
15. sede *om* B
17. intuens O| possimus C
18. bone Jesu LT

19. et *om* B
20. contemplar U
21. tui] tua T
22. tua sola T
23. letari eternaliter LTC
24. quoque] autem L
25. *post* hec *add* in anima L
26. te *om* T| continue U
27. donetur indesinenter L
28. memoria K
29. tui C| dulcedinem K| igitur *om* L
30. *post* qui *add* eructanti K| amore LT
32. Quoniam] Cum T| putant O

Page 13

Line

1. adhuc *om* L
2. Unde et subdit *om* K| et *om* BOU
3. O potentem] Omnipotentem L
4. fundit T
5. instanciam O| perturbare BO
6. nos separabit LU| an^1 *om* T
7. sertus O| sum enim L| enim *om* U| aliqua LTCK
8. sperabit CU| nos separabit L
9. *post* perhibetur *add* quia L
10. enim *om* L
11. veraciter] in veritate BO
13. neque] nec LK
14. describit T scribitur U
17. et *om* U| fallaciam L| agunt no ergo K
18. illa U| deductos BO
19. non timuit se BO
20. fundatum B| *post* qui *add* enim U
21. hebet C

22.   ergo] igitur TU
23.   insolita UK
24.   conabitur U| itaque] ita C ergo L
25.   in domo Dei in eternum U| domo Dei] Domino L| in^2 ...
      speravit] speravit in thesauris pecuniae L
26.   pecunie terrene U| *post* fundatus *add* enim L| sine dubio *om* L
27.   super] supra BOT supra firmam L| in Deo] ideo U
28.   movebitur BOTK| verba B| non *om* K
30.   scilicet] sed L
31.   aliquid U
32.   plenum T| prospicimus T
33.   bene illud L| servimus K| infatigati diu BO| fatigati T

Page 14

Line

1.   statio LTCU
2.   quia] quam L
3.   sine *om* U
4.   quod *om* O
6.   anima et devota U
7.   est] et LTCUK| illud *om* BO| quod *om* U
9.   quis *om* L| iugiter *om* U| *post* Christum^2 *add* recte L
10.   dum vel LTCUK| stando quasi U
11.   oblectari L| celestiam B| est recte BO| recte *om* U| est] et T
15.   vidimus L
16.   gustando T
17.   dulci LTCUK
18.   dulcori C
20.   continuo U| sessione T| *post* Sane *add* igitur K
21.   similima] summa CL| celeste B
22.   plenissima] pe/nissima vita sanctissima U
23.   ad *om* U| hanc] hoc T| amator] amor K
26.   ait] dicit BO| psalmus U| defecit BLC
27.   mea ... vivum *abbr* BO

28. igitur] ergo B| consolamen T
29. fuerit L
33. qui LUK| autem *om* L

Page 15

1. tanto] stando C *om* B| stabilitus L| *post* quanto *add* quasi K| perfectus U
3.   igitur] utique L
4. delcatus U| ficte *om* L| Christum ficte BO
6. fundamentum BO| infirmitur LTCUK
7. a vento . . . ventorum *om* O| radicabuntur O| Et] Similiter CT
9. iusticiam L| bonorum CK
10. suum *om* BO
11. Hic OLTC
12. propheta C| iudicii Dei] iudei O| Non potest enim propheta iustus BO| enim *om* L| potest] fit L
14. est *om* L| quod] qui CL| Et . . . qui^2] quicumque B| Qui^2 *om* U
16. Christi *om* K
18. vero] ergo T| *post* Illi *add* ergo UK
19. et] ac T| quia] quod L
21. *post* moritur *add* mors illi ultra non dominabitur T
22. appropiant T| se *om* U
23. convertatur U| namque namque U| Christi *om* LTCUK| punctio B
24. inveniat LTCU
25. potuerint U
26. impuritate B| quoniam] quando T
28. miseri *om* L| vite presentis L| deditum L
30. infernorum L| nolebant OLTU
31. impletur T adimpleretur L
32. Dominus] deus T| est] ac B autem O

Page 16

Line

1. est *om* LTC
3. gloriam BOL
4. mutaverunt] cantaverunt K| *post* mutaverunt *add* in L| suam]
    Dei BO
7. *post* extra *add* tota L| succendetur K
8. mundana T
9. exarsit K excercerit L| prorsus *om* U
10. que] qui O| ea *om* K
11. inetinguibilis O
12. ante U
13. Gloriatur B| enim *om* B| inquus TK
14. cum conceptam] tamen contemptam L| cupiditatém L
15. veneno si T| haustu BOUK hastu CT| transceditur K
16. noluerat T| argenti L| Si U
17. calidi C calli O
20. perversas *om* B| iudeorum O| Dei] dum BO
21. dum] cum BO| corpora B carnalibus L
23. igitur] ergo K| ab *om* T
24. tutubant L| et] in BOK
25. suis] eius L| inhabentes U
26. et¹] e B| vivere et iuste U| et²] eciam C| sine] sum T
27. placitum BO| unquam T
28. ignis *om* BO
29. devorat L| proponere L
30. ut testatur] inde BO
31. Qui a- amat B| capiat L
32. recte et U| subditur *om* U
33. invenietur T

Page 17

Line

1. quod[1]] quo B
2. amore CL
3. cupedini T| fere T terre L| presumpserunt U
4. amittunt C
5. est *om* BO| pulcritudo ista est L
6. veritas] vanitas L
7. ergo] igitur O| et vane vera *om* BO| oculos solicitans]
   solicitans et oculos L| *post* oculos *add* delectans et U
11. iam *om* BO| iumentis] in mentis C
12. vite] vivencium BO
13. videlicet *om* BO
15. ideo] id est TUK idem CL| per *om* T
16. *post* oppressores *add* et BOU
18. et *om* U| evitent] divitent L| diripiunt *om* O
20. *post* concupiscentiis *add* suis U
21. ipso C| ad illorum] tamen ad aliorum K| ad *om* T
24. quod O
26. pati U| bona] mala BOLCUK
27. *post* faciunt *add* ea L
28. iactant U
29. etiam *om* B
30. summe O
31. denique] enim BO| amatores] dilectores LTCUK

Page 18

Line

3. scilicet] omnibus L| site T| *post* se *add* sed LTCK
4. in infirmitate] infirmitate O in firmitate C infirmitatis L
6. *post* penetrare *add* et BO| Causa] quum T
7. cogiter BO| consilia] coservat B| potuerunt] potest B
8. stabiliri] stabilire T

9.   est L| in] nec CT
10.   vulnere mortis LTCUK
11.   vero] enim T
13.   *post* gemere *add* et BOL
14.   cogitaverunt T
17.   Quod[1]] qui L| eos] es O
18.   suum U *om* B
20.   intendit OLT
21.   sed] et LTCK *om* U
22.   id est] et L
23.   suis *om* C
25.   *post* eius *add* quia L
26.   illecta L| in *om* T| Hic LTCU
27.   torquebunt T
29.   et[2]] etiam U
31.   exaltatum . . . tuis] sanctis tuis exaltatum C
32.   ascendere U ostendere T

Page 19

Line

1.   invisibili gloria C| virtutis L
2.   delectemur CU| hoc *om* L
3.   ipsum laudemus] et B| *post* laudemus *add* et OK

ANNOTATIONS

Page 1

Line

3. Joan. 15. 5
4. quia . . . habemus: cf. 2 Cor. 3. 5.
12. Ps. 84. 9.
16. sed . . . offerre: cf. Eph. 5. 2.
20. Ps. 20. 2.

Page 2

Line

3. Cf. Ps. 20. 2.
9. Ps. 67. 11
24. Dinumerabo . . . multiplicabuntur: Ps. 138. 18.
25. Vere . . . Dei: Ps. 86. 3.
26. memor . . . te: Ps. 86. 4.
30. ante tribunal Christi: Rom. 14. 10; 2 Cor. 5. 10.
30. Non . . . Deus: Act. 10. 34.
32. Gen. 1. 26.

Page 3

Line

2. Ps. 96. 7.
7. atth. 25. 45.
10. demonis gentium: cf. Ps. 95. 5.
12. a nuptiis . . . erit: cf. Apoc. 19. 7,9.
16. iusto . . . rationes: cf. 1 Pet. 4. 5.
22. Joan. 18. 36.
29. regnum . . . mundo: cf. Joan. 18. 36.

32.   in lacum . . . fecis: cf. Ps. 39. 3.

Page 4

Line

1.   ora . . . devoret: cf. 1 Pet. 5. 8.
5.   Ps. 26. 3.
8.   Ps. 20. 2.
13.   Sap. 6. 26.
24.   Ps. 20 . 2.
26.   1 Cor. 13. 5.

Page 5

Line

17.   Ps. 20. 3.
29.   Ps. 20. 3.
32.   Ps. 20. 3.

Page 6

Line

4.   Ps. 20. 4.
14.   gustato . . . Dominus: cf. Ps. 33. 9.
20.   inebriatur . . . Dei: cf. Ps. 35. 9.
27.   Ps. 20. 4

Page 7

Line

23.   Ps. 20. 5.

Page 8

Line

17.   Deus . . . tuam: Ps. 142. 10.
18.   Ure . . . meum: Ps. 25. 2.
23.   Ps. 20. 5.
26.   in mane . . . cogetur: cf. Ps. 89. 6.

28.   quasi . . . permanet: Job 14. 2.

31.   botrus amarissimus: cf. Deut. 32. 32.

32.   Deut. 32. 33.

33.   Ps. 68. 13.

Page 9

Line

2.   Quare . . . videret: Job 10. 18.

3.   Multo . . . discedat: cf. Job 10. 19.

12.   Matth. 10. 22; Luc. 21. 17.

16.   Ps. 20. 6.

30.   Joan. 14. 21-22.

Page 10

Line

9.   Cant. 2. 5.

10.   Ps. 20. 5.

21.   canticum . . . dilecto: cf. Isaiah 5. 1.

Page 11

Line

2.   nec esse . . . vivere: cf. Act. 17. 28.

4.   Ps. 99. 3.

5.   sine . . . agimus: cf. Joan. 15. 5-6.

6.   gloria . . . imponitur: cf. Ps. 20. 6.

12.   Ps. 20. 6.

14.   Ps. 20. 6.

20.   Ps. 20. 7.

30.   1 Cor. 2. 9; cf. Isaiah 54. 4.

32.   1 Cor. 13. 12.

Page 12

4. Funes . . . est michi: Ps. 15. 6.
5. cum . . . ventris: Ps. 126. 3.
6. Ibi . . . est: Ps. 22. 5.
13. in . . . diabolo: cf. Ps. 39. 3.
18. O Jesu bone: cf. hymn *Jesu dulcis memoria*; Cf. Allen 314.
28. memoriam . . . eructanti: cf. Ps. 144. 7.

Page 13

2. Ps. 20. 8.
5. Rom. 8. 35, 38-9.
9. Ps. 20. 8.
10. Ps. 20. 8.
25. qui . . . speravit: Eccli. 31. 8.
26. fundatus . . . petram: cf. Matth. 7. 25; Luc. 6. 48.
28. Ps. 20. 8.

Page 14

11. Igitur . . . prudens: cf. Deanesly, *Incendium*, 185 (See also n. 17, p. xvii.
16. gustato . . . Dominus: cf. Ps. 33. 9.
26. Ps. 83. 3.
31. Ps. 20. 8
33. Ps. 29. 7.

Page 15

5. Sap. 4. 3-4.
10. Ps. 20. 9.
18. Gal. 2. 20.

19. Jac. 2. 20.
20. Rom. 6. 9, 10.
25. quia . . . poterunt: cf. Apoc. 9. 6.
31. Ps. 20. 10

Page 16

Line

4.   qui . . . fenum: Ps. 105. 20.
5.   Pones . . . tui: Ps. 20. 9.
7.   in carcere tenebroso: cf. Sap. 18. 4.
13. Gratulatur . . . malefecerit: cf. Prov. 2. 14.
18. in lacum . . . fecis: cf. Ps. 39. 3.
26. Ps. 20. 10
27. Ps. 20. 10
31. Eccle. 5. 9.
32. Ps. 20. 11

Page 17

Line

5.   Prov. 31. 30.
6.   Cf. Eccle. 1. 2.
8.   Ps. 102. 14-15.
11. Ps. 48. 13.
12. Ps. 20. 11
14. Ps. 20. 12
15. non . . . Deo: Rom. 13. 1.

Page 18

Line

4.   2 Cor. 12. 9.
7.   Ps. 20. 12
11. velut fumus evanescet: cf. Isaiah 51. 6; Ps. 101. 4.
14. Ps. 20. 12
17. Ps. 20. 13

22.   Ps. 20. 13
24.   Matth. 25. 41.
30.   Ps. 20. 14

APPENDIX A

Orthographic Variants

Page 1

Line

3. nihil K
6. magestatis BO
15. quicquid²] quidquid U | quicquid³] quidquid T
16. ridigere T| set L
24. nanque K

Page 2

Line

1. imo K ymo U
14. neglegere T| tremiscunt BOK
18. vidibimus C
20. dispectum Y
25. sivitas C
26. Babylonis K
31. imo UK
32. ymaginem K

Page 3

Line

3. similacris L
4. dispicit T
6. meledictus L
20. latabitur B
24. ymmo B ymo U imo K| dyabolum U| scincera BOLC syncera K
28. dyaboli U

Page 4

Line

7. hillares C

Page 5

Line

1. iucundius K
3. *post* minimum *add* gau L
21. dulcessit BO
24. ymo U imo K

Page 6

Line

1. implisti BC
10. horrere T
12. Quum T
28. laux BO
32. cutta B cunta O

Page 7

Line

12. dyadema LU
13. scitiens C
16. melliffluo K
23. piciit B
28. layci U
29. ocupati C

Page 8

Line

   2.   imo KT

   7.   tollerantium BL

  11.   repparat C

  28.   velud BOLCU (Cf. Annotations, p. 18, l. 11n.)

  30.   imo TK ymo U

  31.   bibebant *abbr* bi. U

Page 9

Line

   2.   dapnatis B

   3.   consumptus . . . videret *abbr* L| tollerabilior BOTCU

   5.   descedat T

  16.   anectit U

  17.   gloria . . . eum *abbr* L| magnum decorem *abbr* LU

  26.   dnante

  32.   dilitescunt BOL dilicescunt T

Page 10

Line

   4.   licorem C

   5.   inmuda L

   6.   Quum LT

  13.   potet L

  22.   *post* dulcore *add* dulc U

Page 11

Line

  21.   *post* seculi *add* le U

  29.   excercitatorum LTCU

Page 12

Line

4.   ceciderut C
9.   iucunditas K| iucunda K
11. desirabilis U
25. aliquatinus C| seperetur B| quomo L
30. gaudiat B
32. Quum T

Page 13

Line

12. discuscione OLU discutione K
24. His K

Page 14

Line

3.   comune C
14. Quum T
17. dulce *mut ad* dulci T
20. conti///e C
31. iucundatur K
32. Altissimi *abbr* BOCU

Page 15

Line

5.   vitlãia O| radices altas *abbr* BO
9.   exerciatur T
10. Inveiatur B| Inveniatur . . . oderunt *abbr* BO
13. set L
20. *post* gravius *add* pec O
21. mortuis . . . moritur *abbr* BO| His L
24. inveietur O
31. Pones . . . devorabit *abbr* O

Page 16

Line

4. ut pote B
5. commedentis O
6. iudiũ B
14. male fecerit C| 9pidinem BO
22. oculatur C

Page 17

Line

1. iniqus C
7. sollicitans BO
12. incipientibus L
16. tyranni K
18. deripiunt B
23. persperitatem *mut ad* prosperitatem T| tollerare C

Page 18

Line

11. velud CU
19. ponit *mut ad* ponet T
23. crucidabuntur C

Page 19

Line

3. gloriomur C

APPENDIX B

The Translation

Here begins the Treatise on the Twentieth Psalm:

Since Christ who is truth says: *Without me you can do nothing*, it is certainly evident that whatever good we either think or will or speak or produce we surely have from God. Let us praise, therefore, and preach the ineffable mercy of the divine majesty and the greatness of His compassion because of which He not only wished to redeem sinners and those sentenced to eternal death but also kindly made clear that we, born and nourished on an island of the great sea, were freed from the jaws of the cursed dragon by the sweetness of the wisdom of the creatrix. Touched by her love and surrounded as if by indissoluble chains, we do not strive for the things of others, but quietly await the grace of our creator, saying with the Psalmist: *I will hear what the Lord God will speak to me.* At any rate, we do not presume to rely upon our own strength, but we trust especially in God to whom we know that we owe ourselves. To Him, I say, we attribute everything from whom we surely have everything; whatever we know, whatever we are capable of, whatever we are, let us strive to return everything to the praise of our creator so that as long as we do not cease with a whole heart, with all our strength, with all our ability to desire the love of God, marked by good character and having been made the masters of our inclinations, we may rejoice in the Lord according to the words of the Prophet: **In thy strength, O Lord, the king shall joy.**

Though all the psalms are sweet and delightful, this psalm especially speaks about the glory of the king, therefore suggesting that no one will joy in the Lord without government, nor anyone be properly guided unless God is his guide. The Prophet therefore describes the joy of the saints and the torment of the wicked, for all of the just and the saints will delight in the explanation of this psalm, but the wicked, who remember that they have acted not well but badly, could be severely frightened.

Thus he is called a king either because he rules or because he reigns; indeed he is more clearly called so because he both rules and reigns. But the king about whom the holy Prophet undertakes to speak – what is it that he rules, over whom does he reign, since he so boldly asserts: *in the strength of the Lord he will joy*? Because in the strength of the Lord neither the king nor the servant will be able to rejoice unless the king will have been found to have ruled rightly, the servant to have obeyed well. Besides, if only kings deserve to joy in God, where do you think servants and the lowly, the despised and the poor will glory? Certainly, let rejoicing without God be called not joy but rather a profane abomination.

The prophet therefore says the same: *In thy sweetness, O God, thou hast provided for the poor*. Now it is clear that God is preparing a place in His sweetness not only for the king but also for the poor man whom He surely sees greatly abased in this world; therefore the conclusion follows that the true poor man will not be called a pauper but a king. Thus by a clear understanding of the word, many who consider themselves kings and rulers are proved to be deceived, as long as they hold the title of king but are not afraid to neglect the task of ruling. For this reason, those who ruled themselves and other subjects badly will fall from their kingdoms destitute. Therefore, O Lord, not just anyone will joy in your strength, but a king – –and not every king.

Who then is the king who will joy? Let us open up the meaning of the word, and we will see that we will speak more fittingly of the just king. O wonderful dignity that a servant of Christ is made a king! For him, to serve is to rule. O piety worthy to be preached; we will see a king despised on earth reigning in God, rejoicing in heaven with the angels! Who ever so repaid his servant, so exalted his soldier, that he made him a king in his court forever! This is the true and eternal king who under him has so many and such great kings wholly aligned with his own will. And lest anyone think that perhaps those so great are few in number, scripture says: *I will number them, and they shall be numbered above the sand. Truly, glorious things are said of thee, O city of God.* Therefore, O good Lord, *be mindful of Raab and Babylon knowing thee* as long as you can be found. For this reason, may it be known clearly in our hearts that before God the wretched man of this world is not despised, nor the honored man taken into account. It does not injure the soul to be downtrodden here, nor does it profit the body to be exalted in earthly things. All the riches, all the delights of this world are counted for nothing *before the judgment seat of Christ. For God is not a respecter of persons,* as is human perversity, or rather the madness of men, which honors the powers of the world not because men were *made to the image and likeness of God* but because they are rich. Hence it is proved that the wretched man shows reverence not to God, nor to men, but to dung – – since riches are called dung by the Apostle. He it is *who adores graven things and who glories in idols,* and he will be confounded since he does not honor the poor man (although he is holy) but rather despises him, thrusts him beneath his feet, and can find no other reason than that he walks in poverty. But listen how unhappy and cursed he is. In wealth he honors dung, in the poor man he condemns Christ. Does he not read and has he not heard: *What you have done to the least of mine, you have done to me?* He is not afraid to offend the poor man all day long; the rich man he desires to please in everything. And look what happens when he does not fear to have Christ angry with him: he joins himself with the gods of the gentiles that are devils. Let every man look to himself, therefore, for unless the man confounded in the nakedness of the shameful will have been clothed in charity, before the eyes of all he will be driven out of the marriage supper of the Lamb and his spouse. But surely he will be the most greatly confounded who is carried from glory to punishment, from riches to poverty.

And so let the sinful poor be afraid, but let the proud rich be more terrified – –because together rich and poor alike will render an account to the just judge. The poor man who perishes is less confounded – –because he was nowhere honored – –than the rich man who once lived wantoning in delights, took pride in his riches, or vainly exalted himself in worldly honors.

Blessed, therefore, is the king who joys in the strength of God, because he indeed will be forever protected from all the confusion of guilt and punishment. But whence is this king and where does he reign since Christ says not only of Himself but in behalf of of His members: *My kingdom is not of this world*? Surely, therefore, it must be obvious that not only the world but the flesh as well is subjected to that king of whom the Prophet speaks. Indeed, he overwhelms even the devil by fighting manfully with a firm faith and sincere charity. The Prophet, seeing this, called him not unworthily, O happy king; and clearly happy is he who has subdued not just one kingdom but four: the kingdom of the world by voluntary poverty, the kingdom of the flesh by sober prudence, the kingdom of the devil by humble patience, the kingdom of heaven by perfect charity! And so his *kingdom is not of this world* because he seeks no joy but from heaven. The ambitious, the greedy, the proud, the extravagant have not conquered kingdoms nor taken castles but were overcome by all of them, and therefore they fall grieving and with justice into the *pit of misery and the mire of dregs* without a kingdom. But he who has destroyed vice in himself has stopped the mouth of *the roaring lion seeking whom he may devour*, despised the world, delivered up the flesh to the spirit; surely such a one is rightly called a king whose power is everywhere obeyed because he did not fear the attacker, continually trusting in God to carry off the victory, crying with the Psalmist: *If armies in camp should stand together against me, my heart shall not fear. If a battle should rise up against me, in this I will be content.*

Let us, therefore, sing joyfully in the praise of God and of his soldier now made king, saying with the Prophet: **In thy strength, O Lord, the king shall joy.** This is the king who rightly rules himself, who constantly directs his body and soul to the service of Christ, who governs all the inclinations of the heart, all the wanderings of the mind, all the desires of the imagination with such control that of the whole being of the inner and the outer man nothing remains that is not disposed to the praise of the creator .

What is said in another place fits that king: *A wise king is the upholding of the people.* The king who gives himself completely to loving

God surely upheld his people. The people of that king are not the men of the earth but the thoughts of the soul which are rightly controlled when all are devoted to the glory of God. Thus the king, ruling himself completely in the love of God and strongly reigning over the stains of every one of the vices, is properly said to joy in the divine strength, who, like a brave soldier, has undertaken to fight off the enemies of Christ. He has certainly been guided by God, and without Him he could not conquer. And so it is well said that he joys in the strength of the Lord and not in his own. For the faithful servant seeks the glory of the Lord so that in his Lord he might also be able to glory.

Indeed, he who glories in the Lord will be glorified by the one from whom he receives everything he has and without whom he could not even exist: **and in thy salvation he shall rejoice exceedingly**. When someone possesses completely what he loves well, then certainly he rejoices exceedingly. For *charity seeketh not her own*, but Jesus Christ. The soul chosen for the salvation of God in Jesus rejoices not only in the future but also in the present as long as it truly and perfectly loves God. O singular gift of love, which alone is borne in fearful ascent to seize the sweetness of the eternal king and deserves to be entertained by the sweetness of such great majesty! For no one finds joy in what he does not love, and this is the reason that sinners never will be able to rejoice in Christ whom they surely never wished to love. But joy is born from the love of the beloved, and some one rejoices more delightfully the more he tries to love Christ fervently. He who loves God before other things will also rejoice more greatly in Christ. He who loves much will joy much, and who loves least will joy least. And he who neglects to love Christ is not able to rejoice completely in Him, so that each of the elect will receive an abundance of blessedness according to the amount of his true love. But the wicked, just as they do not wish to be partners of the lovers of God, so they will not have a share with those glorying in God. But the glory which we will have perfectly and fully in heaven is caused by the charity in which we lived on the way. Thus it is proper that we begin to love here so that we may be worthy to abide in heaven where there is no end of love. Therefore, let us strive to love Christ

with all our might while we are in this present world if we desire glory in the
life to come. The Lord enkindles the hearts of His chosen ones with the fire
of charity, and He supplies to those desiring it what He has foreknown in His
providence is necessary for their salvation. Inflamed by the sweetness of
divine love, they desire only those celestial joys which, because they cannot
obtain them fully in the present, there is no doubt that they will possess
clearly and manifestly from the goodness of God in the future.

Whence it follows: **Thou hast given him his heart's desire: and hast
not withholden from him the will of his lips.** To the king, that is to the saint,
God gave his heart's desire, because that which He wished to give him He
caused him to desire. The saint indeed does not desire, but despises, earthly
things; he seeks not the empty joys of the world but heavenly joys which will
endure without end. He does not love the earth because Christ is sweet to
him. He did not place his desire in the charms of carnal pleasures but fixed
his heart in the enjoyment of spiritual delights. And so God gave him his
desire, indeed gave him more than he was able to desire: He gave him the
society of the angels, the joy of the saints, the blessedness of eternal life, the
seat of eternal rest, the brightness of the true light; He granted him to hear
the angel's song, to see the enveloping light of eternal love, to sing the
honeyed song of delights. What else is there to relate? He gave him full
knowledge of the creator, joy in the whole Trinity. Rightly, O Lord, your
servant upheld his **heart's desire** because **Thou hast not withholden from him
the will of his lips.** For the will is of the lips in the same sense as the desire is
of the heart. He desires with his heart, cries out with his lips, but it is from
the devotion of his heart that the work of prayer ascends to the ears of God.
Therefore **Thou has not withholden from him the will of his lips** but most
mercifully caused it, most abundantly fulfilled it, most richly satisfied it.

But lest anyone think that such great things are done by his own
merits, rather than by the grace of God, it is rightly added: **For thou hast
prevented him with blessings of sweetness: thou hast set on his head a crown
of precious stones.** Justice did not forestall you, O good Jesus, but you
forestalled it with mercy. For unless God with his grace went before the

elect whom He determined to save, He would not find among the sons of men whom He might justify. He inspires one to wish to dwell justly in the blessings of sweetness, He stays close to him so that he might be able to carry out his will. First, therefore, He frightens the man destined to punishments he has merited for his sins so that he might at least stop sinning; and while he avoids committing sins because of the horror of the torments, he begins to a certain extent to correct himself and, so far as his sensuality permits, to desire to do good works. And when he has worked at mortifying carnal desires, a certain taste of heaven in the soul now almost purged begins to sweeten, and, having been tasted, *for the Lord is sweet*, he feels that he has been **prevented in the blessings of sweetness**. So it certainly comes about that he seeks to love or think about nothing but that internal solace. From then on, external things become worthless; he does not trouble himself over wanting or thinking about transitory things or all the empty glory of the world because he judges him alone to be living well and delicately who truly loves Christ. Wherefore, driving out fear, he does not cease to rise to love and, desiring Christ alone, he aspires continually to carry out His will. Now *he is inebriated with the plenty of the house of God* so that no worldly intercourse pleases him; and heated by the fire of the Holy Spirit and melting with the love of eternity, a sweet–flowing fervor overshadows his heart. Inflamed, therefore, by the sweetness of heavenly contemplation, he is more frequently drawn in his mind into that true light; and absorbed by the brightness of divine love and transported from all present things, he is raised to the heights.

Wherefore, of such a man departed from the body or existing in the flesh we sing deservedly to Christ: **For thou hast prevented him with blessings of sweetness: thou hast set on his head a crown of precious stones.** A great glory and no less praise! Above we heard that he joys in the strength of the Lord; now we know that he is crowned in joy, for he receives the crown of imperishable joy, now going to heaven as a victor, who is not afraid to fight bravely and joyfully for Christ. For as long as, disregarding all transitory things, we do not cease to live in the desire for Christ alone, from Christ we do not doubt that we will receive the glory we desire. Moving out, therefore, from this workhouse of present darkness, not unworthily are they gloriously conducted to the light of the heavenly mansions, those who, while they lived in the flesh, tried continually to contemplate with the pure eye of the heart only the joys of heaven. The soldier of Christ, therefore, deserves a crown, not of just anything, but of precious stone, and precious to be sure because it is the reward not only of heaven but of the whole world. That stone is Christ who is the salvation of those who love, the refuge of those who fight, the crown of those who conquer, the glory of those who reign. And so the crown of precious stone is placed on the head of the conqueror, when Christ in the sweetness of the Godhead is shown to the victor. O how sweet and delightful is that king, the saint of God! He deserves to be crowned whom God the Father eternally crowned in His beloved Son. What more could he desire who from the hand of the Lord received so glorious and distinguished a diadem? When the glory of God appears, then hungering, he will be satisfied; thirsting, he will be given to drink; sick, he will be healed; heavy of heart, he will be comforted; conquering, he will be crowned; crowned, he will joy without end. O precious stone, in which all reward is found, without which nothing else is esteemed, which brings the dead to life, raises the overthrown, refreshes the overworked, sows virtues, eradicates vices, comforts souls with the mellifluous joy of love! O precious stone, above gold and all the sweetness of the world I desire it! That stone must be sought with the greatest delight of mind, kept close by continual devotion, embraced with burning love. It must not be put in a coffer but in the soul; let it be hidden in the mind lest it be snatched away by external vanity.

Who loves this stone truly, desires life from God, for which reason there is accordingly added: **He asked life of thee: and thou hast given him length of days for ever and ever.** Here we are openly taught that we must seek eternal life in which we will glory in our heavenly home without end. The saint of God therefore sought life because he desired Christ *who is the way, the truth, and the life* with his whole heart. Now may they groan and languish, tremble and shriek − −all the unjust kings, proud soldiers, wicked rich men, all those, the laymen as much as the clerics, caught up in worldly desire, who do not seek life but prepare death for themselves − − as long as they continue with such great passion and desire acquiring empty honors, tasting passing delights, uselessly possessing riches. For he will die in the bitterness of stench who has lived pleasantly in the delight of carnal love. Nor will he see the divine glory who loved the loftiness of earthly honors. How quickly then does the one chosen of Christ inwardly consider himself and the world, disregarding all visible things, in fact counting them for nothing, and hasten to seek from God only that perpetual and blessed life. For certainly he is excessively blind who fixes his heart on such a treasure which in a short time he knows he will lose. The lover of Christ, therefore, although he suffers a little punishment in this life, nevertheless keeping before the eyes of his heart the celestial glory, is strongly encouraged to endurance by the sweetness of the divine love. Indeed, by as much as the true servant of Christ does not fear to expose himself joyfully to meanness and adversity in this world, by so much more will he be both filled with the grace of love in the present and exalted in glory in the future. The Holy Spirit certainly renews the rejoicing hearts of his own to withstand all suffering for Christ while, extinguishing and casting out carnal desires, it sweetly inflames their minds with the warmth of eternal light. O sweet light, how delightful is the joy which absorbs the souls of lovers in such sweetness that absolutely no weakness of earthly things is pleasing to them now! O Holy Spirit, come and take me to yourself! And well are you called holy who make holy all with whom you have deigned to abide. You are called love, and truly you are the one who always inflames to love those who belong to you. *Teach me to do thy will, for thou are my God. Burn my reins and my heart with your fire*; may that fire burn on your altar. Come, I beseech you, O sweet glory! Come, most delightful sweetness! Come, my beloved! My whole consolation, enter into my soul which languishes for you with a health – giving and sweet – flowing fervor; burn with your fire the inmost parts of my heart; and by illuminating every part with your light consume everything of mind and body with the mellifluous joy of eternal love. To him seeking life from you, our God, **thou hast given length of days for ever and ever** because you have mercifully inspired him to love you, to seek you, to carry out your will. May the poor man who loves Christ rejoice, having one so great and of such a nature dwelling within him.

May he not be frightened if the rich man flourishes and he is punished, and, if in the morning of brief power he is seen to flourish, doubtless in the evening of death and misery he will be forced to wither and utterly fall; indeed, *he cometh forth like a flower, and is destroyed, and fleeth as a shadow, and never continueth in the same state.* The world shows the flower to the fools, but in the end they will not gather the fruit. On the contrary, what appeared to them in the beginning as the flower of sweetness will in the end be perceived as *a cluster most bitter.* Instead of the wine of carnal pleasures which they were drinking, *their wine will be the gall of dragons, and the venom of asps, which is the incurable of torments.* About which Christ lamented, saying: *They that sat in the gate spoke against me: and they that drank wine made me their song.* Surely they will cry out with the damned: *Why didst thou bring me forth out of the womb? O that I had been consumed that eye might not see me!* For it would have been by far more endurable for him if he had been suffocated in his mother's womb than, having come forth from the womb and having received Baptism, to depart again from here enveloped in mortal and actual sins. For rich carousers and tiny aborted infants do not suffer equal punishments. For hellfire will torment the former forever, but the little ones dying without baptismal grace the eternal darkness only will hold. Let him rejoice, therefore, who asks for life, not temporal by which he will have nothing at all, but eternal life in which he may rejoice without end. For surely it is not a part of Christian honor to be exalted among those of earth, but rather to be despised, humiliated, laughed at by the worldly, cursed, and hated as is proved by that passage of the Gospel: *You shall be hated by all men for my name's sake.* So may the lover of Christ, giving up the vain and fallible estates of this world, long continually for the riches of heaven and, suffering joyfully the adversities of this present life, taste indefatigably those interior delights.

In reference to this the Prophet, giving thanks, immediately adds: **His glory is great in thy salvation: glory and great beauty shalt thou lay upon him.** In the salvation of God he certainly gets great glory in Christ who desires Christ with all the love of his heart. For clearly, as long as the holy mind bravely strives to expel from itself the disturbing thoughts of earthly things and does not cease to gather within itself the marks of the virtues, in the sweetness of Christ's love he surely feels great joy. Nor will anyone be able to take joy in the divinity but he who was not too dull to renounce all the vanities and riches of the world. And for that reason his glory is certainly great because he loved much. O love, how praiseworthy you are, how lovable, how desirable without peer when all others have been put aside in comparison to you! In this, moreover, you show yourself strong, powerful, most like a ruler. For whatever man has done, whatever he gave, whatever he suffered, can be rewarded by obtaining temporal goods or by receiving lesser punishments. You are the only one who can be justly rewarded only in the glory of the divine vision. Therefore what Truth said is true: *He that loveth me shall be loved of my Father: and I will love him and will manifest myself to him.* O love, how strong you are who, while they hide behind the vast works of prophecy and miracles by fleeing from the face of Christ, alone do not fear to enter into the court of the eternal king with Christ as your leader, and gloriously you are taken up and with great honor are bid to mount to the throne! Many will see Christ in His humanity but only the lovers of Christ will see Him in the sweetness of His deity. No one takes anything from God for granted – – although he has done much – – because he alone will rejoice in salvation who has loved God. And just as no wise man puts the best wine in a stinking vessel, so Christ, who is the wisdom of God, does not pour His love into an unclean soul. But since the purified soul began to know the sweetness of divine love, it can desire nothing but Christ. It loves Christ, it desires Christ, from Christ it takes fire, it thirsts for Christ, it longs for Christ. It is penetrated by the lance of love and boldly says: *I languish with love.* It is inflamed inwardly by the fire of the Holy Spirit so that it can deservedly sing with the Prophet: **His glory is great in the salvation of God.**

Then indeed the glory of Christ in the faithful soul is great when the soul, charmed by eternal things, cannot be seduced by any glory of the world. For it by reason of the size of its love all temporal things turn to loathing; to it all earthly delight appears a harm so that its glory in Christ may be so great that it can surely find no consolation in this world. Not without cause is solitude proper for him who savors nothing earthly and nothing human. Such a one remains in solitude, of course, because he is far away from men in heavenly conversation. Nor can he be associated with the fellowship of worldly men who only finds delight in the joys of the angels. Sitting alone apart from the tumult but glorying in Christ, he burns and loves, rejoices and sings; wounded by charity, melted by love, filled with the most delightful sweetness, he sings to his beloved the canticle of love. Now he does not say his prayers but, placed in the sublimity of the mind, caught up by the love of the supernal, he is taken beyond himself by a wondrous sweetness and in a wondrous way he is lifted up by God to play upon a spiritual organ. You would not perceive the sound emitted by the corporal instrument because, when the spiritual power overcomes the flesh, the splendor of a good and purified conscience causes it to sing.

A soul of this kind, supported on all sides by so much joy, does not feel injuries, rejoices in abuse, laughs at curses because the soul which only finds delight in the memory of its maker no trouble or misery of this would can shake from love. For logically he is not called just who is not afraid to let the memory of God slip away from him while he watches. But just as there is no place, there is no time, there is no circumstance in which we are not able to feel the kindness of our creator within us, so there is no place, no time in which we may not have God present in memory. So surely without God we cannot subsist, nor exist, nor be moved, nor live; just as when we did not exist, we were not able to create ourselves. Let us therefore say continually: *He made us and not we ourselves.* And just as according to the body without Him we can do nothing, so Him alone we ought to praise for the salvation of our soul because of His grace alone and not by the claims of our merits. For this reason, glory and great beauty are laid upon us when, having despised all the vanities which pertain to the world and the flesh, we glory in God alone. And he who tastes the savor of heavenly sweetness surely cannot find a sorrow that is perverse. Indeed, the bitterness of the world does not punish the heart which the sweetness of Christ refreshes. Over all the folly of this present life, therefore, I have desired the wisdom of God. He who rejoices sweetly in the love of Christ will not see the foulness of hell. If, therefore, in the present *his glory is so great in salvation* that in the place of the fullness of glory he can desire nothing of worldly felicity, how great do you think it will be in the future when God **will lay upon him glory and great beauty?** The blessed soul, drawn out of the body and led to the heavenly kingdom, is bathed in the splendor of divine glory and, rejoicing, is clothed in the beauty of eternal light with the garment of impassibility. But after the general resurrection, glorified in body and soul, shining like the sun but incomparably more brightly, it will enjoy eternal life.

For this reason certainly this appears next: **For thou shalt give him to be a blessing for ever and ever: thou shalt make him joyful in gladness with thy countenance.** This is the joy consummated before the face of God, to dwell in the everlasting seat. He is well given to be a blessing for ever and ever who by contemplating the face of God deserves to be so gloriously made glad. This is the only sight which gladdens the sorrowful, cures the sick, comforts the weak, which truly gives life to all the living. This vision is the joy of heaven, the consolation of the world. In this vision of refreshment they find rest who while they were on the way sustained hard labor for God. O admirable countenance which is the life of the living, the glory of the rejoicing, the light of the illuminated, the rest of the troubled! O sweet joy to see the face of God! O glorious sight to look at the king of the universe in the splendor of his majesty! There will be the joy *that eye hath not seen, nor ear heard: neither hath it entered into the heart of man.* There will be a love most burning, a joy most sweet, a sweetness most abounding when we see God *face to face.* This vision of the holy Trinity is the most complete delight, the most perfect pleasure, the sweetest abundance. O how happy is he who with all his heart strives for it, who with a constant spirit attaches himself to that vision away from all the scorns of the world and the desires of the flesh! O inestimable joy to receive among the angels the inheritance of God! He therefore is able to say with the Psalmist: *The lines are fallen unto me in goodly places: for my inheritance is goodly to me.* For *when he shall give sleep to his beloved, behold the inheritance of the Lord are children: the reward, the fruit of the womb. There is my chalice which inebriated me, how goodly is it!* Where the king is, there is truth and life, law, charity, infinite possession, glory always kept and always longed for. There continually is new enjoyment, enjoyable happiness, happy eternity, eternal security, secure pleasure, pleasing love, beloved vision, the everlasting vision of the creator, desirable fruition. This is what it is to have that blessed life, to possess glory without end. Alas for those who sin briefly and lose that life beyond recovery! Alas for those who desire rather to fall in the pit with the devil by the weight of their sins than to love Christ in truth by living purely and humbly! Therefore are they very fortunate who cross over from the seat of temporal misery to the seat of eternal rest. In these eternal seats surely our joy will be full because, seeing Christ in His beauty, we will be able no longer to gather an increase of glory.

O Jesus, who grants that I may know you, pour yourself into the inmost parts of my soul! Come into my heart and intoxicate it with your sweetness. Fill my mind with the fervor of your love so that, forgetting all evils, I may embrace you alone; certainly then I will rejoice. From now on, do not depart from me because your presence alone is solace to me, your absence alone leaves me sad. Therefore stay with me constantly in my tabernacle, for in your kingdom with you I hope to rejoice eternally. Just as also you are not absent from my memory as long as I will be watchful, so to some extent may the sweetness of your love not be separated from my soul. And just as the soul is disposed to accept no delight but you, so it labors with constant zeal to be given continually to feel your consolation in order that, as long as it does not seek to find pleasure in the vanity of present things, there may be present to the soul proclaiming the memory of the abundance of thy sweetness the sweetness of future things which it desires. Do not be amazed, therefore, if he rejoices who is chosen for the divine love and who is inspired by the joy of supernal things to be a contemplative; but it does not even seem strange if the true lover of Christ, having arrived at death, is more greatly delighted because he does not expect to die but to live, since he is not unaware that he goes to Christ whom alone he has desired.

This certainly is the king of whom the Prophet is not afraid to speak further and whom he boldly affirms is worthy of such great honor. Whence he adds: **For the king hopeth in the Lord: and through the mercy of the most High he shall not be moved.** O mighty king who makes His servants kings and establishes them so firmly in the belief that no instance of trouble is permitted to disturb them! Whence the Apostle: *Who shall separate us from the love of God? Shall tribulation? Or distress? Or the sword? Or famine? Or nakedness? For I am sure that neither death, nor life, nor any other creature shall separate us from the love of God which is in Christ Jesus.* Rightly therefore and truly is he said to hope in the Lord and in the mercy of the most High, who will not be moved from that event which hope awaits. For many say they hope in the Lord, and in truth they do not hope, but truly they lie because in fearful shaking they will clearly show evil deeds, not hope in the Lord but despair. And therefore, because such men are not kings nor hope in the Lord, they cannot stand but will be shaken and perish. Besides, it is written clearly enough that the king, that is, the just man hoping in the divine mercy, who has desired to be fixed in God, the immutable and immovable good, is not moved because whoever is not fixed in God is employed in fallible and fleeting things. But plots against nature do not work; they therefore deceive all those dedicated to them. It is fitting then that such a man fall who did not fear to establish himself in falling things. Certainly in the desires of present riches there is a fragile and deceptive foundation: who clings to them is sure to be moved. For he has a place of rottenness who has placed the foundation of his mind in acquiring earthly things. The worldly wretch who has always tried to gather up vain and unreliable, unjust and superfluous things will justly be shaken by his desires. When these things fall, how fortunate is he who cannot be moved, who will abide in the house of God for ever. *He it is that hath not gone after gold nor put his trust in money nor in treasures*; he was founded without doubt upon rock, i.e., he has rooted the end of his desire in Christ; made steadfast in God, he will not be moved with this world. Much can be said about this phrase: **he will not be moved,** but for now these few words may suffice.

We have three things from the kindness of creation with regard to the body, namely: to run or to walk, to stand and sit. If we look at some sight while running, it is clear that we do not perceive it plainly because we have been too much moved. Standing, however, we see it well, but, because we cannot stand for a long time unfatigued, we do not doubt that standing is not much different from motion. But sitting, we will be able to see it clearly, and seeing, we can find delight because it is common enough to sit and it can be done for a long time without running or standing. For, if anyone had someone he knew loved him a great deal, he was accustomed to sit close to that person that he loved much a great deal, not to run or stand. God is surely the object of the soul from its natural beginning; therefore the faithful and devout soul desires to have nothing but God before its eyes. Where the love is, there surely is the eye. For that which we especially love we incessantly long to see and possess. And so, since he loves Christ, he continually desires to be raised up to see Christ. But as long as he is distracted by earthly things, as if running, or as long as he is still less pleased to contemplate heavenly things, as if standing, he by no means is properly wise. Sitting, therefore, and keeping quiet, the soul becomes prudent. Hence certainly it is clear that the soul which faithfully and truly fixes the love of Christ in itself and before its eyes now does not cease to draw its body to a seat. Thus, since we begin to love God by first hating our sins, there can be no doubt that, unless we see Him as if while running, after having tasted that the Lord is sweet, we all at once leave the things of this world behind; and so the spirit of Christ entering into us as sweet as honey, enticed by the greater delight, we stand as if to see God. But finally inflamed by the sweetness of eternal love, raised up too to the joy of song, we desire incessantly the quiet of mind and body so that, continually sitting, we may rejoice in the perpetual vision. Clearly this is the life most perfect, most holy, and most like that of the angels, but also the life most full of heavenly sweetness which I think anyone among men can comprehend. Certainly very few attain it. In it, however, the ardent and perfect lover of Christ is most truly recognized if he through the whole course of a night and day is delighted to sit. For the divine love compels him to be quiet so that the whole man might be filled with the joy of heavenly sweetness. For this reason the Psalmist says: *My soul longeth and fainteth for the court of the Lord. My heart and my flesh have rejoiced in the Living God.* Do not wonder, therefore, if he is able to sit perpetually who has been so sweetly intoxicated by the consolation of celestial joys. For, sitting, he sings and rejoices and is often taken up by the sweetness of heavenly love and, strengthened by the contemplation of eternal things, he is wondrously delighted. Wherefore the Prophet justly cries out of this: **For the king hopeth in the Lord: and through the mercy of the most High he shall not be moved.** He cannot be moved because he is rooted perfectly in God. Thereafter in another place it is said: *And in my abundance* (i.e., of charity) *I said: I shall never be moved.* For everyone of the elect is situated more securely to the degree that he is rooted more perfectly in true love.

I am not surprised therefore if, beaten by temptation, he quickly falls who was not delighted and surrounded by the true love of God. Whence it is most truly said of those who pretend to love God: *Bastard slips shall not take deep root, nor any fast foundation. And if they flourish in branches for a time, yet, standing not fast, they shall be shaken with the wind, and through the force of winds they shall be rooted out.* And lest anyone think that the goodness and mercy of God is so great that His justice is not exercised against the wicked, behold he turns his discourse at once from the glory of the blessed that has been described to the punishment of the wicked, saying: **Let thy hand be found by all thy enemies: let thy right hand find out all them that hate thee.** This is the prophecy and delight of the just judgment of God. For the just Prophet cannot wish that sinners and wastrels should live in their iniquities. But you must know that there are enemies of Christ. And who are they? Those who hated Him; surely those who hate are enemies. And by no means does anyone have an enemy by whom he is not hated. The enemies of Christ, therefore, are the false Christians who are now trying to kill in their hearts the Christ whom they received in Baptism. Otherwise Paul would not have said: *But Christ liveth in me.* They do not have Christ living in them but Christ destroyed and dead in their sins because *faith without works is dead,* and they sin more seriously than the Jews crucifying Him. But surely *Christ, rising from the dead, dieth now no more. But in that he liveth, he liveth unto God.* Indeed, death and misery draw near to them since their grief and iniquity might be turned upon their heads. For the judgment of God will be found by the enemies of Christ and eternal punishment will find them because they will die in torments without end, and they will never be able to die who wished to live always in their sins, offending God.

And so no one of sound mind imagines with impunity that a mortal sin which is not forgiven in this life, when found by the hand of God, will be punished in hell without end. Wherefore, as long as wretched mortals, given to the vain cares of the present life, desire to cling to earthly gains they fall grieving, losing the joys of the world which they had loved, to the fires of hell which they wished to avoid so that what now follows may be fulfilled in them: **Thou shalt make them as an oven of fire, in the time of thy anger. The Lord shall trouble them in his wrath: and fire shall devour them.** This is the punishment of His enemies, this is the punishment of those who hate Christ. Alas for sinners! Alas for those wishing to sin whose riches are turned to poverty, health to death, delights to foulness, beauty to ugliness, sweetness to bitterness, glory to fire – –and deservedly inasmuch as *they changed their glory into the likeness of a calf that eateth grass.* **Thou shalt make them as an oven of fire, in the time of thy anger.** O hard lot of the sinner when he shall come to judgment! In all his being within and without, the flames of hellfire are enkindled and, condemned to eternal miseries, he is confined in a dark prison forever. And justly is he, who as an oven will have been kindled by the fire of worldly desire as long as he was concerned with present riches, drawn completely away from those things which he had loved to those which he did not fear, putting an end to prayers, will be always burning in the conflagration of inextinguishable fire so that, swallowed up by the abyss of eternal death, he is much more displeased by his torments than ever before he had been able to please himself in the enjoyment of his sins. For the wicked man rejoices when he has done evil and when he knew he could fulfill the desire of lust which he had conceived; he is pierced not a little way by the stubborn spear of the poisonous serpent so that, having forgotten the judgments of God, he is induced by a burning desire to commit the evils he had wished.

And so, as long as he was not afraid to give assent to the temptations of the crafty deceiver, he voluntarily submerges his own soul in the pit of misery and mire of dregs. This of course is bad, indeed the worst, that we see when we restrain our perverse desires and thoughts neither by the fear of God's judgments nor the sorrow of torments; but as long as pleasure is set before our bodily eyes, the condemnation of the most just judge is completely hidden from the consideration of the heart. Therefore the wicked, perceiving the sweetness of carnal desires, driven far from all spiritual joy, now beaten to earth by a hard death, stagger; and clinging only to their earthly pleasures, they think nothing is more foolish than to live innocently and justly. For which reason and not without deserving **shall the Lord** whom they never desired to please **trouble them in his wrath.** And fire shall devour them, i.e., hellfire shall devour them whom the fire of extravagance and passion had first devoured. Undoubtedly, such wretches, because they joy in placing earthly before heavenly things, having counted all their good works for nothing, will despair after death, as the wise man testifies: *He that loveth riches shall reap no fruit from them.*

Whence there rightly is added: **Their fruit shalt thou destroy from the earth; and their seed from among the children of men.** Alas wretched fruit! After it has been lost, sorrow is found; having lost what it loved, the world will mourn; having found what he did not expect, the wicked man will be tormented. The lovers of the world flourish in youth while they give themselves up to carnal love and earthly desire; but when they dare to bear fruit, they will lose all flower and fruit. The flower of the world seems sweet, but, lest it sweetly bear fruit, it is quickly cut down. O how *deceitful is that favour and how vain that beauty!* What is a flower of carnal beauty but an empty truth, and true vanity is truly called completely transitory. Vain therefore is all the glory of the world, truly vain and vainly true, tempting the eyes and intoxicating the soul with a poison cup. We do not recall: *that we are dust. Man's days are as grass: as the flower of the field so shall he flourish.* Look at the flower of the field and you will be able to find the flower of this kind of man. In fact, carnal man has been made like vanity because of his sin and *compared to senseless beasts,* and therefore his fruit, namely the fruit of life, is destroyed from the earth; and his *seed from among the children of men,* that is, of those people living good lives, is scattered because of his guilt.

And justly indeed: **For they have intended evils against thee; they
have devised counsels which they have not been able to establish.** Against
you, therefore through you, because there is no power but from God. Surely
tyrants, perverse rich men, oppressors of the poor, wicked princes, and how
very many others, even robbers, although they take what belongs to
others – – wherefore they prosper in carnal delights and avoid the adversities
of the world – – nevertheless they acquire them only through God, i.e.,
through the power given by God, however much they may have a bad will
from their desires. And if they are entirely opposed to the will of the creator,
He bestows on them temporal goods for their destruction.   Sinners,
therefore, and wantons turn aside from God into evils surely because they
refuse to endure with a whole heart the adversities of the world because of
the prosperity given them by God. For we see that all lovers of the world
altogether shun thirst, hunger, and cold as much as they can; and if they will
have been tempted, they do not stand but fall. Thus it is certainly evident
that they flee from and hate the good deeds which hasten to heaven, and they
love and do the evil deeds that lead to hell. O foolish and irrational
merchants who, while they boast that they are enriching themselves by
avoiding punishment, show themselves most poor and wretched before the
most high judge, not only deprived of all good but cast down into the depth of
evil!

The lovers of Christ, then, love what the lovers of the world hate; for
they even find joy in taking up for Christ the calamities of the present life,
but doubtless in Christ's name they desire to shun all evils, that is to say,
those things which are vices and defilements of the soul; in other words, they
constantly avoid sins by the love and help of Christ as long as they know that
in other evils, namely hunger, thirst, cold, nakedness, they are being
tormented for their own good because, if *power is made perfect in infirmity*,
surely he who is perfect in power is free from all infirmity. Worldly wretches,
therefore, avoid evil badly because, while they think they escape evil, they
never stop falling into the evils of hell. The reason is in the text: **For they
have devised counsels which they have not been able to establish.** For the
proud man will not be able to be established in his pride because Lucifer,

who was prideful in heaven, was suddenly dashed into the pit of hell. Nor will the rich man find support in his wealth, but, when he has been struck by the wound of a hard death, all the glory of his house *shall vanish like smoke.* Neither will the carnal lover, serving the pleasures of the flesh, be able to sport in a steady course because the flesh will fail, ugliness will take him over, a merciless death will carry him off so that afterwards the sinner is forced to groan, no longer to exult. So surely: **They devise counsels which they are not able to establish.** For the counsels of the wicked will not stand, but rather will perish in the judgment of the king of the ages.

This is noted in what follows: **For thou shalt make them turn their back.** Rarely is that which is put behind the back remembered. God therefore will put His enemies back because He will not intend ever to look back at those condemned to the sorrow of eternal fire, dispossessed of the mercy of His compassion. And as if put behind His back and completely forgotten, the damned will not feel solace, but, as if they were always before the face of the avenger, they will grieve. **In thy remnants thou shalt prepare their face,** i.e., their bodies along with their souls will be tormented with the demons when the irrevocable sentence has been fulfilled on them, according to which it is said: *Depart from me, ye cursed, into everlasting fire, which was prepared for the devil and his angels.* As many illicit pleasures as they had in this world, just as many everlasting torments will they have in hell. Here it is clearly shown that evil men will be tortured among the demons.

Surely the company of the saints will rejoice among the choirs of angels. Just as the Prophet states their glory and exultation in the beginning, thus confirming it at the end, he says: **Be thou exalted, O Lord, in thy own strength: we will sing and praise thy power.** Just as he said: Show yourself exalted in your saints whom you made in your power to ascend above every earthly thing. For certainly, as long as we are divinely seized by the love of invisible glory, we will delight to sing and praise from our hearts the mighty works of the power of God. And in the present through grace and in the future through glory, may we love Him, praise Him, and glory in Him for ever and ever. Amen.

Bibliography

Albertus Magnus. "Commentarius in Psalmos," *Opera Omnia*, ed. A. Bourgnet. 38 vols. Paris, 1890-98.

Alford, John A. "Biblical Imitatio in the Writings of Richard Rolle." *ELH, A Journal of English Literary History* 40.1 (1973): 1-23.

Allen, Hope Emily. *Writings Ascribed to Richard Rolle Hermit of Hampole and Materials for His Biography.* New York: Oxford UP, 1927.

Bonaventura. "Expositio in Psalmos," *Opera Omnia*, ed. A. C. Peltier. 15 vols. Paris, 1867.

Boenig, Robert. *Richard Rolle: Biblical Commentaries.* Salzburg Studies in English Literature. Austria: University of Salzburg, 1984.

Clark, J. P. H. "Richard Rolle as a Biblical Commentator." *Downside Review* 104 (1986): 165-213.

_____. "Richard Rolle, A Theological Re-assessment." *Downside Review* 101 (1983): 108-139.

Corpus Christianorum, Series Latina. Turnhout, Belgium, 1963.

Donne, John. *The Anniversaries*, ed. Frank Manley. Baltimore, 1963.

"Duns Scotus," *New Catholic Encyclopedia.* 1967. Vol. IV.

Everett, Dorothy. "The Middle English Prose Psalter of Richard Rolle of Hampole," *Modern Language Review*, XVII (1922), 217 seq. and 337 seq. and XVIII (1923), 381 seq.

Hahn, A. *Quellenuntersuchungen zu Richard Rolles englischen Schriften.* Berlin, 1900.

Horstman, C. *Yorkshire Writers: Richard Rolle of Hampole and His Followers.* 2 vols. London, 1986.

Jorz, Thomas de. *Commentarius super Psalmos.* Venice, 1611.

Lapide, Cornelius a. *Commentarii in Scripturam Sacram.* 10 vols. London, 1864.

Lubac, Henri de. *Exégèse Médiévale: Les Quatre Sens de l'Ecriture.* 2 vols. Paris, 1959.

Noetinger, Dom. "The Biography of Richard Rolle," *The Month,* January, 1926.

Quetif, J. and J. Echard. *Scriptores ordinis Praedicatorum,* ed. R. Coulon. Rome, 1910.

Rashdall, Hastings. *Universities of Europe in the Middle Ages.* 2 vols. Oxford, 1895.

Rolle, Richard. *The Fire of Love or Melody of Love and the Mending of Life or Rule of Living,* ed. Frances M. Comper. London, 1914.

_____. *The Incendium Amoris of Richard Rolle of Hampole,* ed. Margaret Deanesly. Manchester, 1915.

_____. *The Melos Amoris of Richard Rolle of Hampole,* ed. E. J. F. Arnould. Oxford, 1957.

_____. *Officium de Sancto Ricardo de Hampole,* ed. G. G. Perry. Early English Text Society, Original Series No. 20. London, 1867.

_____. *The Officium and Miracula of Richard Rolle of Hampole,* ed. R. M. Wooley. London, 1919.

_____. *The Psalter or Psalms of David and Certain Canticles with a Translation and Exposition in English by Richard Rolle of Hampole,* ed. H. R. Bramley. Oxford, 1884.

_____. Selected Works of Richard Rolle of Hampole, ed. G. C. Heseltine. London, 1930.

Schneider, J. P. *The Prose Style of Richard Rolle of Hampole, with especial reference to its Euphuistic tendencies.* Baltimore, 1906.

Smalley, Beryl. *The Study of the Bible in the Middle Ages.* Notre Dame, 1964.

Spicq, C. *Esquisse d'une histoire de l'exégèse latine du moyen age.* Paris, 1944.

TEXTS AND STUDIES IN RELIGION

22. James Gollnick, *Flesh* as Transformation Symbol in the Theology of Anselm of Canterbury: Historical and Transpersonal Perspectives

23. William Lane Craig, The Historical Argument for the Resurrection of Jesus During the Deist Controversy

24. Steven H. Simpler, Roland H. Bainton: An Examination of His Reformation Historiography

25. Charles W. Brockwell, Jr., Bishop Reginald Pecock and the Lancastrian Church: Securing the Foundations of Cultural Authority

26. Sebastian Franck, Sebastian Franck: 280 Paradoxes or Wondrous Sayings, E. J. Furcha (trans.)

27. James Heft, S.M., John XXII and Papal Teaching Authority

28. Shelley Baranowski, The Confessing Church, Conservative Elites, and The Nazi State

29. Jan Lindhardt, Martin Luther: Knowledge and Mediation in the Renaissance

30. Kenneth L. Campbell, The Intellectual Struggle of the English Papists in the Seventeenth Century: The Catholic Dilemma

31. William R. Everdell, Christian Apologetics in France, 1750-1800: The Roots of Romantic Religion

32. Paul J. Morman, Noël Aubert de Versé : A Study in the Concept of Toleration

33. Nigel M. de S. Cameron, Biblical Higher Criticism and the Defense of Infallibilism in 19th-Century Britain

34. Samuel J. Rogal, John Wesley's London: A Guidebook

35. André Séguenny, The Christology of Caspar Schwenckfeld: Spirit and Flesh in the Process of Life Transformation, Peter C. Erb and Simone Nieuwolt (trans.)

36. Donald E. Demaray, The Innovation of John Newton (1725-1807): Synergism of Word and Music in Eighteenth Century Evangelism

37. Thomas Chase, The English Religious Lexis

38. R. G. Moyles, A Bibliography of Salvation Army Literature in English (1865-1987)

39. Vincent A. Lapomarda, The Jesuits and the Third Reich

40. Susan Drain, The Anglican Church in Nineteenth Century Britain: Hymns Ancient and Modern (1860-1875)

41. Aegidius of Rome, On Ecclesiastical Power: De Ecclesiastica Potestate, Arthur P. Monahan (trans.)

42. John R. Eastman, Papal Abdication in Later Medieval Thought

43. Paul Badham (ed.), Religion, State, and Society in Modern Britain